JOSHUA

JOSHUA

The Conquest of Canaan

KEN FLEMING

MINISTRIES
The Word to the World

Joshua: The Conquest of Canaan
Ken Fleming

Copyright © 2006 ECS Ministries

ISBN 1-59387-057-4

First Edition 2006

Published by:
  ECS Ministries
  P.O. Box 1028
  Dubuque, IA 52004-1028
  www.ecsministries.org

Cover: Ragont Design, Barrington, Illinois

All rights reserved. No part of this book may be reproduced or transmitted in any form or by any means, electronic or mechanical, including photocopying and recording, or by any information storage and retrieval system, including the Internet, without the prior written permission of the publisher, with the exception of brief quotations embodied in critical articles or reviews.

All scripture quotations, unless otherwise indicated, are taken from the *New King James Version.* Copyright © 1979, 1980, 1982 by Thomas Nelson, Inc. Used by permission. All rights reserved.

Printed in the United States of America

Contents

Introduction 9
<u>Joshua</u>
  1. The Commission to Joshua 17
  2. Rahab and the Spies 29
  3. The Crossing of the Jordan..................... 37
  4. The Memorial Stones 47
  5. The Base Camp at Gilgal 55
  6. The Destruction of Jericho 65
  7. Defeat at Ai 73
  8. Victory at Ai.. 81
  9. The Treaty with Gibeon 91
  10. Victory in the South 97
  11. The Northern Campaign and Final Victory 107
  12. Conquered Kings and Cities 115
  13. Division of the Land East of Jordan 119
  14. The Inheritances of Caleb and the Tribe of Judah ... 127
  15. The Boundaries and Cities of Judah's Inheritance ... 131
  16. The Inheritance of Joseph 135
  17. Issues Relating to Manasseh and Ephraim 139
  18-19. The Distribution of Land at Shiloh 143
  20. The Cities of Refuge 151
  21. The Levitical Cities 157
  22. A Crisis Averted 161
  23. Joshua's Farewell Address to the Leaders 167
  24. Joshua's Farewell Address to the People 173

Maps

The Land of Canaan 7
The Southern Campaign 98
The Northern Campaign 108
The Distribution of Land 118, 126, 144
The Cities of Refuge 150

Introduction

THE MAN JOSHUA

Joshua does not suddenly appear on the pages of Scripture after the death of Moses; several references to him appear in the books of Exodus and Numbers. A consideration of these passages will help in understanding the human character of Joshua and the process by which God prepared him for leadership.

Although Joshua and Moses were different in character and temperament, there are some interesting similarities between the two men. Like Moses, Joshua was eighty when he began his major life work. Both were great leaders of the people of Israel. Moses led Israel out of Egypt and across the Red Sea to Sinai where they corporately received God's Law; Joshua led Israel out of the wilderness, across the River Jordan, and into the Promised Land where they corporately renewed their commitment to obey God's Law.

Scripture divides the lives of both Moses and Joshua into three periods. Moses' 120 years were comprised of:

- forty years in Egypt training to be a leader
- forty years in the desert learning to know God
- forty years leading the Israelites out of Egypt and in the wilderness

As for Joshua, he spent:

- approximately his first forty years as a slave in Egypt learning to suffer with God's people
- the next forty years as Moses' assistant in the wilderness learning the ways of God and the skills of leadership
- his last twenty-five to thirty years leading the Israelites into their God-given inheritance

Joshua's Personal Background

Joshua came from a prominent family in the tribe of Ephraim although, according to 1 Chronicles 7:20-21, there were cattle thieves among his ancestors! His father's name was Nun. Joshua is called "the son of Nun" some twenty-nine times. His grandfather was Elishama, the captain and leader of the tribe of

Ephraim at the time of the exodus (Num. 2:18). Like all the Hebrew men living in Egypt, Joshua would have worked as a slave making bricks for the Egyptians. From early childhood he would have learned of the covenant promises God had made to the patriarchs that the sons of Israel would come out of Egypt with great possessions and inherit the land of Canaan. From time to time he would have seen the unburied casket of his ancestor Joseph awaiting its long-promised removal to the homeland (Gen. 50:25).

Joshua's Growing Anticipation of Deliverance

In his youth, Joshua would also have heard of Moses, the Israelite who had grown up as a prince in Pharaoh's palace. Some had hoped that Moses would deliver Israel but, after killing an Egyptian, he had fled east. Joshua would have heard that Moses had returned to Egypt after a forty year absence saying that God had commanded him to tell Pharaoh to liberate His people. Pharaoh however, would not let the Israelites go, resulting in Jehovah sending a series of plagues and judgments on the Egyptian people.

After nine such judgments Moses and his brother Aaron told the children of Israel that the final plague would be the death of every firstborn child in the land. The angel of death completed his work: every firstborn child of homes not protected by the blood was struck dead, including the firstborn son of Pharaoh. As a result, Pharaoh ordered Moses to immediately take the people out of his country. The Israelites, some two million of them, were prepared, and they left in haste. As they began to journey into the wilderness, Joshua would have been aware that his tribe of Ephraim had the responsibility of carrying Joseph's mummified body in a coffin back to the Promised Land (Ex. 13:19). His grandfather, Elishama, led the entire tribe of Ephraim, consisting of 40,500 people, out of Egypt (Num. 1:32).

Experiences that Shaped Joshua

With all of the other Israelites, Joshua perceived God's guiding hand in His provision of the pillar of cloud and fire to lead them out of Egypt (Ex. 13:21). He discerned the power of God displayed as the Red Sea opened before them. He joined in the praise of the people as they responded to the songs of Moses and Miriam. He witnessed the bitter waters of Marah being changed into sweet drinking water. He ate the manna God provided from heaven to feed the people. And when they murmured because they were thirsty, Joshua saw Moses strike the rock from which water gushed out for all to drink. These experiences would have fully convinced Joshua that God was with them.

Experiencing the Hand of God in Battle (Ex. 17:8-16)

During his wilderness experience, Joshua received a significant leadership opportunity which God used to prepare him for his role in conquering Canaan.

Following the incident when Moses struck the rock from which water gushed out, the stragglers at the rear of Israel's traveling multitude were attacked by the Amalekites at Rephidim. It is here that we first meet Joshua in Scripture. "And Moses said to Joshua, 'Choose us some men and go out and fight with Amalek'" (Ex. 17:9). At this crisis point, Moses appointed Joshua to the role of army general. It was a challenge to the Israelites—especially Joshua—for the people had no military experience. But Moses went on to tell Joshua, "Tomorrow I will stand on the top of the hill with the rod of God in my hand" (v. 9).

When Joshua had chosen his men and was prepared for battle, Moses held up his rod from his vantage point on the top of the hill. As long as he did so, Joshua's men maintained an advantage over the enemy. When Moses became tired, Aaron and Hur helped him by supporting his hands until the sun went down. The incident closes with: "So Joshua defeated Amalek and his people with the edge of the sword" (v. 13). Joshua learned from the Battle of Rephidim that deliverance and victory do not come from man's effort or skill, but from the Lord—a lesson that proved valuable when he became Israel's leader. From Numbers 13:16 it appears that Moses changed his given name from Hoshea, meaning "salvation," to Joshua, which means "Yahweh is salvation," so he was thereafter constantly reminded that *God* was his deliverer.

Witnessing the Glory of God on Mount Sinai (Ex. 24:9-18)

When they reached the base of Mount Sinai, God commanded Moses, Aaron, Nadab, Abihu, and the seventy elders (of whom Joshua was one) to climb up the mountain. When they were part of the way up they saw the God of Israel, and under His feet was "a paved work of sapphire stone . . . like the very heavens in its clarity" (v. 10). It was similar to the vision that Ezekiel saw hundreds of years later. This vision of God, however it may be explained, was absolutely incredible, and the seventy elders expected to be killed. However the next verse tells us that God did not "lay His hand on them" to judge them; rather, they ate and drank. The elders, together with Aaron, Nadab, and Abihu, remained part way up the mountain, while Moses with his assistant Joshua went higher.

Joshua stayed with Moses on the mountain of God for six days covered by a cloud while the "glory of the Lord rested on Mount Sinai" (vv. 13-16). The children of Israel on the plain below said that it looked "like a consuming fire on top of the mountain." On the seventh day God called Moses to continue up the mountain alone, leaving Joshua there in the cloud for the next forty days (v. 18). For Joshua, the vision of God on a pavement of sapphire, the consuming fire glowing through the thick cloud, and the forty days meditating alone in that cloud while awaiting the return of Moses with the tables of stone must have been a life-changing experience. He learned there something of the glory, holiness, and power of God.

Worshiping in the Tent of Meeting (Ex. 33:11)

Forty days later, following the incident of the Golden Calf (Exodus 32), God told Moses to lead the people into Canaan, but He would not go with them (33:3). The people began to repent and Moses set up a tent outside the camp as a place to meet with God, called the Tent of Meeting. As the people watched him go in, they saw the pillar of cloud standing at the tent indicating God's presence. There God spoke to Moses "face to face." Joshua was with Moses in the tent, and he was so overcome by God's presence that he would not leave, even when Moses did. Joshua learned the value of being in God's presence and of worshiping Him.

Accepting the Ministry of Others (Num. 11:24-29)

After they had left Sinai, Joshua complained to Moses that two men, Eldad and Medad, were prophesying in the camp. In Joshua's opinion, Moses was the only man with the right to speak for God, so he asked Moses to forbid them to speak. But Moses corrected Joshua, saying, "Are you zealous for my sake? O that all the LORD's people were prophets and that the LORD would put His Spirit upon them" (v. 29). Joshua learned not to be jealous when God uses others. It is God's prerogative to choose who will serve Him. Joshua discovered that the servants God chooses to use are not necessarily the people's choice.

Standing against the Drift (Num. 13-14)

The Israelites proceeded north and arrived at Kadesh Barnea on the border of the Promised Land. The Lord told Moses to choose leading men, one from each of the twelve tribes, to "spy out the land of Canaan." Joshua was chosen to represent the tribe of Ephraim. When they returned and gave their report, only Joshua and Caleb believed that God would indeed give Israel the victory over the Canaanites. The other ten saw themselves as "grasshoppers" by comparison with Canaan's fortified cities and armed soldiers. But Joshua and Caleb declared, "If the LORD delights in us, then He will bring us into this land and give it to us, 'a land which flows with milk and honey.' . . . The LORD is with us. Do not fear them" (14:8-9). The congregation of Israel, however, did not listen to them. They sided instead with the ten spies and sought to stone Joshua and Caleb on the spot. Joshua learned about standing up for what you believe to be true and that the majority is not always right. In this regard Joshua was in the line of some great Christian leaders, like Huss, Luther, Knox, Wilberforce, Booth, and Carey.

Being Anointed by the Holy Spirit (Num. 27:12-23)

Thirty-eight years later, in the plains of Moab, God told Moses that he would not be allowed to lead the people across the Jordan and into the Promised Land (Num. 20:12). Moses prayed that God would "set a man over the congregation . . . who may lead them out and bring them in, that the congregation of the LORD may not be like sheep which have no shepherd" (vv. 16-17). God answered Moses' prayer with, "Take Joshua the son of Nun with you, a man in whom is the Spirit, and lay your hand on him." Moses then took Joshua and set him before the priest and all the children of Israel, and he laid his hands on him (vv. 22-23). Joshua learned that he needed the power of the Spirit of God to lead God's people (cf. Acts 6:3-5).

Relying on God for Wisdom (Deut. 34:7-8)

When the Israelites arrived at the border of Canaan, the Lord took Moses to the top of Mount Nebo from where he was able to view the Promised Land. Moses died there in Moab, and the Lord buried him. Scripture says, "Now Joshua the son of Nun was full of the spirit of wisdom . . . so the children of Israel heeded him" (Deut. 34:9). Joshua learned that no one is indispensable and that the wisdom he would need to do the task God had assigned him would come from God alone.

Summary

In these seven passages God gives us insight into how He prepared Joshua to become the leader of the Israelites during the conquest of Canaan. God uses similar means today to prepare those whom He will use in His service. Many of these separate incidents were small in and of themselves, but in each one Joshua learned an important lesson while proving himself faithful to God. Together these events demonstrate that the man God chose was both well prepared and highly qualified to serve as a leader.

THE BOOK OF JOSHUA

Having learned something of the man Joshua we can turn with greater insight to the book. The storyline concerns the events surrounding the Israelite invasion of Canaan and the partitioning of the land among the twelve tribes. The people were emerging from forty years in the wilderness. As their new commander, Joshua was to lead a military invasion, conquer Canaan, and settle the twelve tribes of Israel there.

Authorship and Date of the Book

The question of who wrote the book of Joshua has been the subject of much debate among Bible scholars. Although it is written anonymously, one statement near the end of the book indicates that Joshua wrote at least some of it: "Then Joshua wrote these words in the Book of the Law of God" (24:26). While it may be that "these words" refer merely to the covenant words at Shechem and not the whole book, evangelical scholars generally believe Joshua wrote most of it and that others added the details concerning his death and a few later events. Chapter 6 must have been completed during the lifetime of Rahab, the woman of Jericho, for it says "she dwells in Israel to this day" (6:25), indicating that she was still alive when the book was written. Evangelicals generally cite the biblical evidence to support an early date and believe that archeology can be interpreted to support that stand. Liberal scholars, on the other hand, have generally placed its writing after the monarchy was established by David and Solomon, while some think it was written after the exile. They interpret archeological evidence to support their position and generally reject internal biblical evidence.

Most evangelicals date the exodus about 1445 BC (with good reason), thus dating the beginning of the invasion of Canaan at about 1405 BC and the writing of the book of Joshua near the end of his life, twenty-five years later (in approximately 1380 BC). A discussion of the questions surrounding the dating of Joshua is beyond the scope of this commentary. We will accept the reasoning of evangelical scholars, believing that Joshua wrote the majority of the book and that it was completed by others after he died.

The Historical Setting

The land of Canaan extended from Gaza in the south to Sidon in the north and from the Jordan River on the east to the Mediterranean Sea on the west. It comprised about 8,000 square miles (9,200 square kilometers), roughly the size of the State of New Jersey in the United States or one half the size of Switzerland in Europe. When the people of Israel (numbering probably about two million) entered Canaan, the Middle East was controlled by three powerful civilizations. To the north of Canaan, the Hittites lived in what we call Turkey today. To the east, the Babylonians occupied the Euphrates River Valley. To the south, the Egyptians inhabited the Nile Valley. Between these three powers, smaller groups of unstable city-states like Canaan existed. However, during the time of Joshua, neither the Hittites nor the Egyptians were trying to expand their influence, leaving a power vacuum in Canaan. The Israelites exploited that situation when they invaded the land.

In the context of biblical history, Joshua grows out of the books of Moses. During their forty years in the wilderness, Moses had prepared the Israelites for their inheritance of the Promised Land. Not only had he been an outstanding leader and lawgiver, he had also written the five books of the Pentateuch to communicate to them their history from creation to their becoming a people and a nation. Moses had imparted to them the Law from God which taught them their responsibilities to Him in daily life and worship. Moses had reviewed all these things in the book we call Deuteronomy while they were preparing to enter Canaan, just before he died.

Joshua's Three Purposes for Writing

While not specifically stated, we can observe three purposes that Joshua appears to have had in mind when he wrote the book. The first purpose was to demonstrate the fulfillment of the promise to Abraham that his seed would inherit Canaan. That promise was first given when Abraham was still in Haran (Gen. 12:1-3) and confirmed to him when he separated from Lot (Gen. 13:15). God later defined the borders of the land and named all the peoples that his descendants would displace when they came to live there (Gen. 15:18-21). Later still, God told Abraham that Canaan would be his descendants' everlasting possession as part of an established covenant (Gen. 17:8). After Abraham's death, God confirmed the promise of the land to Isaac (Gen. 26:3). He reiterated it later to Jacob at Bethel before he went to Haran and when he returned twenty years later (Gen. 28:13; 35:9-12). All three of the patriarchs were buried in the land at Hebron. Later, when Joseph was dying in Egypt, he commanded that, when his people returned to the land, they were to take his bones with them and bury them there (Gen. 50:24-25). Thus, when Joshua wrote of the conquest of Canaan, it was in direct fulfillment of a whole series of prophecies to the patriarchs.

Joshua's second purpose was to encourage the Israelites to complete their conquest of all the land of Canaan after he was gone. He had demonstrated that God had been faithful to His promises, granting them the land by His grace, sovereign will, and power, and not by their own military power or skill. For this reason Joshua wrote of how God miraculously caused the walls of Jericho to fall down and of when the sun stood still. If they understood that the land they inherited was a gift from God and a fulfillment of His promise to Abraham over five hundred years earlier, it should have been a natural step to trust that God would be faithful to give them the rest of the land.

Joshua's third purpose was to demonstrate that God was holy and righteous. It was only when God's people obeyed His word that He gave them victory and blessing. The first twelve chapters of Joshua are far more concerned with obedience to God's covenant than with the details of the battles fought. It was the ark of the covenant and the activity of the priests that were central to their obedience in the crossing of the River Jordan. They were obedient in setting up memorial stones in the river and on the Canaan side at Gilgal. They were obedient in renewing the rite of circumcision as the sign of their covenant with God. They reinstituted the keeping of the Passover. Even when they "attacked" Jericho, it was their obedience to God's command to march around the city that resulted in God causing the walls to crumble. Blessing came from their obedience, but judgment came because of disobedience. Achan's disobedience in taking of the forbidden goods at Jericho led to their defeat at Ai. Joshua's record would have taught the children of Israel that God would bless them when they obeyed and judge them when they did not.

Illustrations in Joshua

The book of Joshua is more than interesting Bible history and more than an exhortation to the Israelites to claim the Promised Land. It provides us with wonderful illustrations of spiritual truths for believers (1 Cor. 10:11). Canaan is an illustration of the "heavenlies" or "heavenly places" that the apostle Paul wrote of in his letter to the church at Ephesus in the New Testament. Believers have been blessed with many spiritual blessings (Eph. 1:3). However, these blessings, like the blessings of Joshua's people, are enjoyed only if they are *claimed.* They are to be claimed in the arena where spiritual battles take place and where spiritual victories are won. They are the portion of our inheritance that is for life on earth today. The pagan strongholds of Canaan illustrate the enemies that Christians "wrestle" against, such as "principalities . . . powers . . . the rulers of the darkness of this age . . . spiritual hosts of wickedness" (Eph. 6:12). The Israelites fought against seven enemy peoples named as the Canaanites, Hittites, Hivites, Perizzites, Girgashites, Amorites, and Jebusites (3:10). These peoples lived in fortified strongholds like Jericho, Ai, Gibeon, Libnah, Lachish, Hebron, and Gaza. The spiritual warfare of the believer parallels the offensive war in which the Israelites were engaged.

Joshua, as their leader, pictures the Lord Jesus Christ. The name *Jesus* in the Greek language is the same as *Joshua* in Hebrew. Jesus is the "greater Joshua" who leads His people into their inheritance, just as Joshua did. The book of Hebrews speaks of Joshua as a "type" of Jesus. It is Jesus who has given His people rest which is greater than the rest Joshua gave the people who followed him (Heb. 4:8). The Lord Jesus leads His people; He is the Captain of their salvation.

Two Phases of the Conquest

The conquest of Canaan was to be completed in two phases. The first phase was a united campaign where all available Israelites fought together as a large army to defeat the major strongholds of their enemies. First they attacked the central region; then they moved to the south as far as Gaza; finally they conquered the north as far as Mount Hermon (Joshua 1-12). Up until this time, no one was allowed to settle in the land. After that, the land was divided among the twelve tribes and the families were allowed to settle in the cities and farms of the area where each tribe was assigned. The second phase of the plan for each tribe was to secure its own territory and settle there (Joshua 13-24). The wise Bible student will gain a much better understanding of these latter chapters by frequently referencing the maps provided in the commentary.

Having reviewed the setting, purpose, and ways in which God prepared Joshua to lead the Israelites into Canaan, the reader will be better able to profit from a study of the book itself.

Joshua 1

The Commission to Joshua

The Israelites were at an important juncture in their national and spiritual history. Over a twenty-five year period they would enter, conquer, and occupy the Promised Land, the territory that we call Israel today. There has been—and continues to be—a great dispute over which people group has the rights to this land. The Muslim world argues that the followers of Mohammed occupied the land in AD 638 and that it was inhabited by various groups of Muslims for most of the next 1310 years (until 1948). The Israelis who gained control of part of it in 1948 stake their claim on God's promise to Abraham and on the actual invasion of the land by the children of Israel under Joshua's leadership in 1405 BC, more than 2,000 years before the Muslims came. The Jews and their descendants have maintained a presence in the land (albeit sometimes a very small presence) ever since they conquered the land under Joshua. Throughout that long period of history, many enemies have wanted to evict them. Their present day enemies, the Palestinians, are part of a much larger struggle by the Muslim nations of the world to regain control of the land and drive them out.

The first chapter of Joshua is about God's command to Joshua to cross the River Jordan into Canaan. It includes God's promise that every place they trod on was to be their own possession and that no people in the land would be able to stop their advance. Finally, it records God's encouragement to Joshua to be strong and courageous in light of faith in God's promise and obedience to His Word.

"Moses . . . is dead" (v. 1)

The book of Joshua begins as the sequel to the story of Moses that was brought to a close in the previous chapter in our Bible, Deuteronomy 34. Moses knew the Lord "face to face" and was used by Him to perform unprecedented signs and wonders (cf. Deut. 34:10-12). However, God was not dependent on Moses. Even after Moses died, God continued working in the world, and especially among His chosen people. As the saying goes, "God removes His workers but He carries on His work." God removed Moses but carried on His work through Joshua.

Joshua—Israel's New Leader

As instructed by the Lord, Moses transferred his authority to Joshua by placing him before the priest in the presence of all the people (Num. 27:18-20). He then placed his hands on Joshua, signifying the transfer of authority and blessing. At that time Joshua was filled with the spirit of wisdom, and the people recognized him as their new leader (Deut. 34:9). The order is important: it begins with God's choice, followed by man's acceptance and obedience. Moses did not die of weakness or old age. God removed him and buried him to make way for Joshua, their new leader.

Moses was not the only one to die. The entire adult generation that had left Egypt forty years earlier died in the wilderness because of their rebellion against God at Kadesh Barnea. Because they refused to believe that God could give them the land, God told them that they would not enter it. It was thirty-eight more years before everyone over twenty-years-old when they left Egypt had died, the only exceptions being Caleb and Joshua (the two spies who had courageously believed that God would indeed give them the land). Thus it was with good reason that God chose one of them to be the Israelites' new leader.

Joshua, the Servant of Moses (v. 1)

God described Joshua as the "assistant" of Moses (v. 1). He held this position for forty years. There is an important principle about leadership for us here. Many inexperienced people want to jump into leadership positions without first having learned to serve behind the scenes in lowly positions. The person God uses must first learn to be a servant. Joshua spent forty years in training as Moses' assistant before God designated him as a leader. Even after Moses laid his hands on him he did not rush out and command the army to invade Canaan. He waited for God to speak and direct him.

When Joshua is referred to as "Moses' assistant" there is a deliberate contrast with the term used to describe Moses: "the servant of the LORD." This phrase is used to describe Moses three times in this chapter (vv. 1, 13, 15). Moses is referred to as "the servant of the LORD" thirteen times in the book of Joshua, but it is not until the very last chapter that the title is used of Joshua himself (24:29). It would seem that Joshua earned that title by his life of obedience and faithfulness to God. This is especially significant, because the title is only used of one other person besides Moses in the Old Testament—David.

"Arise, go over this Jordan" (v. 2)

With Moses gone and Joshua in place as the new leader, the time had come for the nation to move forward and possess their inheritance. God said, "Now therefore, arise, go over this Jordan . . . to the land which I am giving to them." It was something to the effect of, "Get up on your feet, get over the obstacle of the River Jordan and get into the land of blessing on the other side." We all face these kinds of situations that call for commitment and obedience. The time for thinking and counsel is past. No more seminars on the strategy of invasion, or how to prepare kosher food, or a twelve-step program to victory. If they believed that God was going to give them the land, they needed to put their feet where they said their faith was, so to speak.

Christians today often talk and sing about being soldiers for Christ and gaining victory in Jesus. However, talking the good talk is much easier than fighting the good fight. C.T. Studd, a well known missionary of the late 19th century, found the same was true in his day, and he wrote a parody on the hymn "Onward Christian Soldiers" to motivate believers to become missionaries. He wrote,

> "Mark time, Christian heroes, never go to war;
> Stop and mind the babies playing on the floor."

The commission God gave Joshua was to "you and all this people" (v. 2) — not to Joshua alone, but to the entire nation. So we as believers must arise with our Leader, the greater Joshua, and "possess the land" of victory and blessing that is before us.

The first two verses emphasize the fact that God was *giving* the land to the Israelites. The word *give* is used almost seventy times in Joshua in connection with the land and its parts. God was the primary Giver. God gave the land to the nation of Israel to fulfill His promise to Abraham, Isaac, and Jacob. The basis for God giving them the land was His love: "Because He loved you . . . He brought you out of Egypt . . . driving out from before you nations greater and mightier than you . . . to give you their land as an inheritance" (Deut. 4:37-38).

The Strategy (v. 3)

The *giving* of the land by God is balanced with the *taking* of the land by Israel. "Every place that the sole of your foot will tread upon I have given you." The land was theirs, but they had to possess it step by step. God had promised that their victory would not be instant or sudden. Exodus 23:30 says, "Little by little I will drive them [the enemies] out before you, until you have increased, and you inherit the land." That was the strategy, but they had to put it into action. This step-by-step strategy is also the way to spiritual blessing and victory. We do not become mature Christians overnight; when we follow Jesus He leads us into victory after victory over sins like pride, jealousy, stubbornness, disobedience, and lack of faith, one at a time.

The Israelites on the east side of the Jordan looked westward toward Jericho and saw the fruitful land during harvest. The grain was waving in the wheat fields and the vineyards were heavy with grapes. However, possessing it was only a tantalizing possibility until they actually crossed the river and took possession of the fields one by one. The further in they went, the more they would see what could be possessed.

The people were willing to follow Joshua, but relatively few believers today are willing to follow the greater Joshua into the spiritual inheritance that is available for all of us. The tragedy is that most Christians go home to heaven having never really "possessed" or enjoyed all that God wanted to bless them with while here on earth. These are the ones who remain unwilling to leave their worldly and fleshly ways. And because they do not identify themselves with the death and resurrection of Christ in a practical sense by putting to death the deeds of the flesh and living in the reality of His resurrection power, they do not fully experience their new life or obtain victory over their spiritual enemies. Rather, they spend most of their lives on the border as defeated Christians, seldom entering into "the land" of spiritual victory. The New Testament tells us to follow the example of Joshua by *laboring* to enter into that rest (Heb. 4:11).

The Extent of their Inheritance (v. 4)

God gave Joshua a detailed description of the land. The southern border was the wilderness through which they had come on their way from Egypt. The northern border is described as "this Lebanon," the same mountain range that is in the modern country of Lebanon. The eastern border was the River Euphrates and the western border was the Mediterranean Sea. All the land between the east and the west was called the "land of the Hittites." The word *Hittite* as used here is simply another word for the Canaanites, even though there was a large kingdom of peoples called Hittite in Asia Minor at about the same period of history. The borders described here are far larger than the land that was occupied by the Canaanite peoples. Actually, the people of Israel have never yet possessed it all, although they came close to doing so at the end of David's life (1 Kings 4:21). There is a day coming, however, when Israel will fully occupy all the land that God has deeded to them (Jer. 16:14-16; Amos 9:11-15; Zech. 8:4-8). We too are blessed with all spiritual blessings in the heavenlies (Eph. 1:3) and have a vast inheritance in Christ.

Victory Based on the Presence of God (v. 5)

God wanted to encourage Joshua in his huge responsibility to lead the people into a hostile land. Fortified cities with trained armies would fight for every inch of it. God promised him that no enemy would be able to stand before him. He said, "I will be with you. I will not leave you nor forsake you." In guaranteeing His presence, God gave Joshua a most convincing historical example: "as I was with Moses" (v. 5). Joshua knew well of God's presence with Moses through the ten plagues, the Red Sea, the wilderness, hunger and thirst, attacks, grumbling, and unbelief. Through it all God had been with Moses, and He would be with Joshua. God promised continuous victory as long as he lived. It is equally true that He will be with us. If God is for us, who can be against us (Rom. 8:31)?

Fear not I am with thee, Oh be not dismayed,
For I am thy God, I will still give thee aid,
I'll strengthen thee, help thee, and cause thee to stand,
Upheld by my gracious, omnipotent hand.

Rippon's *Selection of Hymns*
"How Firm a Foundation"

The Courage to Conquer (vv. 6-9)

The story of Joshua is an allegory of how the people of God can move from their mediocre Christian experience to a victorious Christian experience as they possess their inheritance in Christ. Just as the Lord encouraged Joshua, so He encourages us to follow Him into the place of blessing. Our inheritance, like Israel's, will not be easily achieved. Their inheritance was in enemy territory with fortified cities and giants. Our inheritance is in the heavenlies, where principalities and powers and the rulers of the darkness of this age try to stop us from obtaining spiritual victory over such enemies as sin, doubt, fear, and trials. The thought of conquering their enemies made the Israelites afraid. Without God it is easy to let our fears and our failure to trust God keep us from enjoying all that He has for us. The "day of small things" mentality has gripped far too many people, where we become resigned to accepting second best (cf. Zech. 4:10).

"Be strong and of good courage" (v. 6)

In the first few verses, God commanded, "Get up . . . get out . . . get over . . . get into." Between verse 6 and the rest of the chapter, the words "be strong and of good courage" occur four times (vv. 6, 7, 9, 18). The Israelites—like us—needed strength because they were weak, and—like us—they needed courage because they were afraid. As their leader, Joshua would need courage more than anyone in Israel. Leading people into new territory is always difficult. When people do not share the same vision and drive that their leader has, they are slow to follow. They quickly sense fear, turn back, and are quick to complain.

The Reasons to be Strong and Courageous

Each time God called Joshua to be courageous He gave him good reason to be so, indicated by the little word "for" which occurs each time the command was given. The first "for" is in verse 6 and relates to the people: "Be strong and of good courage, *for* to this people you shall divide as an inheritance the land which I swore to their fathers to give them" (v. 6). The second "for" occurs in verse 8 and relates to God. With respect to keeping His Law, God said, "*For* then you will make your way prosperous, and then you will have good success." The third "for" appears in verse 9 and relates to Joshua himself: "*For* the LORD your God is with you wherever you go." Let us pursue these three calls to courage a little more deeply.

- Joshua could have courage in light of his role in *the purpose of God* to give them the land (v. 6).
- Joshua could have courage in light of the provision of *the written Word of God* (vv. 7-8).
- Joshua could have courage in light of the assurance of *the presence of God* (v. 9).

Courage in Light of the Purpose of God

The first call to be strong and courageous was given because Joshua was to divide, as an inheritance, the Promised Land. It takes courage to lead people into their *spiritual* inheritance. Have you ever tried to teach someone who thinks they are under law, not grace (Rom. 6:14)? Have you ever tried to teach eternal security in Christ when a person thinks they have to personally "hold on" to their salvation? Have you ever persuaded someone to put into practice the biblical discipline of personal prayer? Most believers are "dull of hearing" and want only "milk" instead of the "meat" of the Word of God (Heb. 5:11-14). God gave the land to Israel, but it was only theirs to enjoy when they appropriated it.

Believers, pictured by the nation of Israel, are to be possessors, not just surveyors. The twelve spies had been surveyors of the land from one end to the other, but they ended up possessing nothing except a large bunch of grapes. Joshua needed to be strong and resolute to bring the people into the land, but he could be so because he knew he was fulfilling God's purpose.

Courage in Light of the Word of God

The second reason for Joshua to be courageous was that he had the Word of God which he was to carefully obey. This time God told him to be *very* courageous, because it would take more courage than claiming and dividing the inheritance (vv. 7-8). The context gives us the reason for this: it always takes more courage for leaders to deal with their own personal obedience than to exhort others to obey. Joshua was told he must "observe to do according to all the law which Moses my servant commanded you . . . then you will have good success." The instruction manual was the law God had given to Moses. Joshua was responsible to personally obey *all* of it.

The reference to Moses in verse 7 is interesting. Moses had received the Law from God and had just completed writing the first five books of our Bible. Even though he was gone and many things for the Israelites were changing, no change was to be made in the Law or the standards of conduct that God demanded. For example, He had declared, "Be holy, for I am holy," and this command was not to change just because the standards of the world had changed (Lev. 11:44). Fifteen hundred years later the same moral standard was just as applicable to the readers of Peter's letter (1 Pet. 1:16). The great moral principles of God's Word do not change.

The Responsibility to Obey

Notice several aspects about Joshua's responsibility to obey (vv. 7-8). He was responsible to obey the entire law. The commandment was "observe to do," or "be careful to do." He needed to be determined and resolved to know all the Law and to put it into practice. It was not enough for him to pick out a favorite section and find comfort in it. It was not enough to know the truth of creation or offer occasional sacrifices. Instead, he was to know and observe the entire Law.

God told Joshua to obey the spirit of the Law, not just the letter of it. He was to do "*according* to all the law" (v. 7). He did not need a specific verse for every word or action. The spirit of the Law, which refers to those things that are consistent with the written Law and that result in God's glory, would guide his decisions and actions. For God's people, although many areas of life are not specifically addressed and discussed in Scripture, we can still find guidance in the *spirit* of Scripture. "All Scripture is given by inspiration of God, and is profitable for doctrine, for reproof, for correction, for instruction in righteousness" (2 Tim. 3:16).

Joshua was also responsible to be consistent. He was not to deviate from it either to the right hand or to the left (v. 7). Some people can be scrupulous about certain biblical commandments and ignore others. Joshua was commanded to run a straight course of complete obedience.

Meditation

The Book of the Law was not to "depart" out of Joshua's "mouth," meaning he was not to forsake it. Whenever he spoke, Joshua was to use Scripture as the basis of his authority and as a tool for communicating wisdom and instruction to the people. God told Joshua, "You shall meditate in it day and night." Meditation is quiet contemplation of God and His Word. We often liken it to the practice of a cow chewing the cud. The repetitive nature of meditation is an excellent, character-building habit for believers; sadly it is a lost art among most of us. Constant noise and various forms of distraction rob us of the quiet heart meditating on the Word of God. Just as, in many ways, "we are what we eat" physically, so "we are what we eat" and digest spiritually. Jeremiah said, "Your words were found, and I ate them, And Your word was to me the joy and rejoicing of my heart" (Jer. 15:16).

The Hebrew people, however, had a slightly different concept of meditation. To them, their thoughts were accompanied by the reciting of the actual words out loud. The basic meaning of the word "meditate" is to "mutter," which reflects this habit. For this reason God charged Joshua, "This Book of the Law shall not depart from your mouth" (v. 8). He was to be constantly repeating it aloud. This form of meditation remains a practical way of keeping focused on the subject at hand. Many Christians make a habit of praying aloud for the same reason.

Prosperity and Success

God promised Joshua that if he kept the Law he would prosper wherever he went and would have good success (vv. 7-8). A number of Christians today use this passage to promote what is known as the "prosperity gospel." They believe that if they honor God in their lives and keep His commands, He will prosper them financially and materially. It may be an attractive idea, but it is decidedly unbiblical. Some of God's choicest saints have never experienced material prosperity. Even the Lord Jesus Christ had nowhere to lay His head (Luke 9:58). The words "prosperity" and "success" as used here in Joshua are not used in the Bible for material or financial gain; rather, they refer to prosperity and success in the legitimate pursuits of life. For Joshua, success would be in leading the Israelites into their inheritance. Many biblical references to success link it with obedience to God's Word (e.g. 1 Kings 2:3; 2 Kings 18:7).

The key to Joshua's success was to be in observing to do according to all that is written in the Law. He set his heart on God and strived to do His will. When he understood the will of God, he carried it out faithfully and fully. And in obeying the will of God, he enjoyed success.

Courage in Light of the Presence of God

The third reason why Joshua was to be strong and courageous was that Jehovah God was with him. No matter what might happen, he did not need to fear, because God's presence was with him. The human temptation is to be afraid when situations seem beyond our control. Joshua was not to be afraid, even when he stood outside the massive walls of Jericho, or when he saw the heavily armed giants. Like Joshua, we can take courage knowing that God is with us wherever we go.

Joshua's Command to the Officers (vv. 10–11)

With God's encouragement, Joshua assumed direct leadership of the Israelites. He gathered the "officers" of the people together to instruct them. In all probability, these men were not army officers but tribal officials. They were part of an organized chain of command that could be used to spread orders quickly and efficiently. From the outset, the invasion was to be a matter of obedience to God rather than one of military expertise.

Joshua told the officers to "command the people, saying, 'Prepare provisions for yourselves, for within three days you will cross over this Jordan, to go in to possess the land.'" Notice how they were told to prepare themselves: they were to gather "provisions," that is, grain and fruit from the surrounding fields in Moab to add to the manna which God continued to provide until they actually crossed over the Jordan. Nothing was said about sharpening their swords or stringing their bows for war. Again, their preparation involved simple obedience to the command which was spiritual, not military, in nature. Victory in Canaan was to be God's victory, not the Israelites', and possession of the land was God's gift, not a result of their military prowess. But although God had already given them the land as an inheritance, they would still have to cross the Jordan to possess it. The word "possess" is used twice in this verse to emphasize its importance as the central idea of the book of Joshua.

Three Days

Joshua told the people that within three days they would cross over the Jordan (v. 11). A slight interpretive problem exists in connection with the term "three days" as another three-day period is referred to in Joshua 3:2. How can these two three-day periods be reconciled?

The best solution appears to be that the first "three days" refers to a time of preparation before leaving their camp on the plains of Moab that lay between the hills of TransJordan and the River Jordan. The place where the people actually stayed was called Shittim, where they had camped since their encounter with the prophet Balaam and the defeat of the kings Sihon and Og (2:1; 3:1; cf. Num. 21:21-22:1). During these first three days, the spies were sent to Jericho and returned. Having heard the report of the spies (2:24), Joshua made plans regarding the order in which the Israelites would cross the Jordan. At the end of the second three-day period, the people sanctified themselves and prepared to cross on the seventh day (3:2, 5).

Joshua Gives Instructions to the East Jordan Tribes (vv. 12–15)

The focus now moves to the Reubenites, the Gadites, and half the tribe of Manasseh. Before Moses died, the Israelites had fought the Moabites and Midianites and had encamped on the plains of Moab (Numbers 31). These 2½ tribes possessed very large domestic herds. After observing that the nearby land of Gilead was especially good for grazing, they asked Moses if they could have it as their inheritance, saying, "Let this land be given to your servants as a possession. Do not take us over the Jordan" (Num. 32:1-5). Then they offered to fight alongside the other 9½ tribes when they crossed the Jordan and invaded Canaan. They promised, "We will not return to our homes until every one of the children of Israel has received his inheritance" (Num. 32:18). Moses agreed that if they kept this arrangement they could have the land of Gilead as their inheritance but warned them that if they did not, "Be sure your sin will find you out" (Num. 32:20-23). In other words, they would suffer some consequences if they failed to follow through on their commitment. The east Jordan tribes promised that "every man armed for war" would cross over with the others until the job was finished (cf. Deut. 2:26-3:12-22).

The Duty to Remember Previous Promises

Joshua now reminded these 2½ tribes of their earlier commitment (v. 12). The word "remember" is the key word: "Remember the word which Moses the servant of the Lord commanded you . . . your wives, and your little ones, and your livestock shall remain . . . on this side of the Jordan. But you shall pass before your brethren armed, all your mighty men of valor, and help them, until the Lord has given your brethren rest" (vv. 13-15). The idea of *rest* signifies that there would be peace with their enemies and that their borders would be secure. Rest mentioned here for the first time in Joshua is repeated sixteen more times in the book. It becomes a key theme in Joshua. This idea also appears in some of the prophetic passages regarding their life to come in Canaan (cf. Ex. 33:14; Deut. 8:20; 12:10). Joshua told the east Jordan tribes that when the tribes west of the Jordan had found rest, the east Jordan tribes could return to their inheritance and enjoy it.

Of significance is Moses' instruction to send "all" their fighting men to come and help. It should be noted that, when the people were numbered, there were 110,580 men capable of bearing arms from these tribes (cf. Num. 26:7, 18, 34). However, we read in Joshua 4:13 that only 40,000 of them actually crossed the Jordan. A lesson gleaned from this observation is for the need for wholehearted commitment to fulfill a promise.

Israel Responds (vv. 16-18)

After speaking to the officials and to the 2½ tribes, the grammar in verses 16-18 indicates that the response to Joshua's words came from all Israel, not just the ones he had been addressing in verses 10-15. They affirmed that they would faithfully obey Joshua in whatever he told them to do: "All that you command us we will do, and wherever you send us we will go" (v. 16). It was a strong and enthusiastic pledge of allegiance and commitment to serve in any capacity.

The people went on to say, "Just as we heeded Moses in all things, so we will heed you." Although the people were sincere in their commitment, in actuality they had neither heeded Moses in all things nor accepted all the words of God through him. The book of Numbers lists ten occasions when they grumbled and complained (cf. Num. 14:22). One example of their disobedience occurred when they promised Moses, "All that the Lord has said we will do, and be obedient" (Ex. 24:7). A little while later they made a golden calf while he was on Mount Sinai with God (Ex. 32). The entire wilderness journey is filled with examples of Israel's disobedience and rebellion. The people continued in their response to Joshua by admitting this tension when they added, "only the Lord your God be with you" (v. 17). Because they knew that God, at least, would prove faithful, they added to their words of well-intentioned commitment, "only the Lord your God be with you, as He was with Moses."

We need to learn that we should be honest with ourselves and others about our past testimony and be careful about making sweeping and unrealistic promises as to future actions.

The Discipline for Rebellion

The Israelites went on to emphasize their commitment to Joshua's leadership. They vowed that any small infraction or disobedience on their part would be met by severe punishment. That person, they said, "shall be put to death," because the disobedience would be viewed as rebellion. The phrase, "Whoever rebels against your command," is literally "whoever rebels against your mouth." The phrase is also found in Deuteronomy as "rebellion against the command [or mouth] of the Lord" (cf. Deut. 1:26, 43).

This degree of severity was in line with military discipline. The death penalty was carried out against Achan when he deliberately sinned against Joshua's command (Joshua 7). In the final statement, the people urged Joshua to "only be strong and of good courage" (v. 18), the same statement with which God had exhorted Joshua three times (vv. 6, 7, 9).

In Conclusion

Israel's captain was now Joshua. Joseph had saved the budding nation from starvation. Moses had delivered them from bondage. Joshua would lead them to victory. By picturing Joseph, Moses, and Joshua as types of Christ, we can experience the truth of all three in our Christian lives, and usually in that order. Christ first saves us from sin; He then delivers us from the power of the world; finally, He leads us into the place of blessing and victory.

Joshua 2

Rahab and the Spies

The first chapter of the book of Joshua records the Lord's clear command to prepare for the invasion of Canaan. All the people agreed unconditionally to follow Joshua's leadership until they had taken possession of the land. Chapter 2 continues the story of preparation for the invasion by recounting a single episode about two spies whom Joshua sent to Jericho to assess the strength of the city and to bring back an accurate report.

The Encampment at Shittim

The Israelites were still encamped at Shittim, a few miles from the River Jordan, and this would be their last encampment before crossing the river and entering Canaan. The name *Shittim* is translated "Acacia Grove." It was at Shittim that Balaam the prophet had persuaded Israelite men to marry Moabite women and join them in making sacrifices to the Moabite god Baal. The Lord judged them severely by sending a plague that killed 24,000 of them (Num. 25:1-9). Israel had learned that they could not trifle with God's Law. They were still in Shittim when Moses died on nearby Mount Nebo (Deuteronomy 34).

Ten to fifteen miles separated the Israelites in Shittim from the walled and heavily fortified Canaanite city of Jericho, which lay to the west against the hills on the other side of the river. A large flowing spring supplied Jericho with ample water, as it does to this day. No doubt its watchmen had been apprehensively observing the movements of the huge encampment for some time. From Rahab's testimony we know that they had heard stories of the Israelites' flight from Egypt, their crossing of the Red Sea, and that God was credited with giving them victory over the powerful kings, Sihon and Og, on the east side of the Jordan (v. 10).

Joshua Sends the Spies (v. 1)

As Joshua looked westward across the river, it was obvious to him as a general that before any foothold in Canaan could be secured, he would have to defeat Jericho. The city guarded the hills and valleys that provided access to the remainder of Canaan. And because God had commanded Joshua to conquer

Canaan, Jericho would have to be taken first. Yet although Joshua was fully committed to following God's directions, he did not yet know all the details of God's plan. He did, therefore, what any commander would do: he sent spies across the river to find out all they could about Jericho's fortifications and defenses, telling them, "Go, view the land, especially Jericho." Several commentators have interpreted this move by Joshua to be an act of impatience on his part, an unwillingness to wait for God. However it is better to see his sending of the spies as an example of faith in action. He was obtaining the most up-to-date and accurate information he could, rather than simply waiting for another divine revelation. Many of God's people would be well advised to follow his example. When Joshua needed information, he sprang into action and commissioned spies to gather it. Initiating logical and sensible steps does not negate faith, because faith should always be complemented by active obedience.

Joshua's full name, the son of Nun, is used here. The use of this name often indicates a new section in the story. Note its use in the beginning of both chapters 1 and 2 (cf. 2:23; 19:49; 24:29). The shorter name, Joshua, appears much more often (over 130 times). This new section deals with the sending of the spies. Notice that it specifically says that he sent them to spy *secretly*, an unusual expression, as spy missions are inherently secretive. He may have been trying to keep the mission a secret from his own people. Perhaps he was concerned that the men might bring back a negative report, just as the ten spies had from the previous spy mission in which Joshua himself had participated (Numbers 13-14). If so, he might have been anxious that once again the spies' report would cause the people to rebel. Whether or not this is the case, he certainly did not want word of the spies to reach Jericho, whose citizens would be on the lookout for them.

Rahab's House (vv. 1-2)

Despite the spies' efforts to keep their presence a secret, they were seen entering the house of Rahab, a harlot. It appears that fear of the Israelites had already gripped the people of Jericho, including their king, who immediately sent soldiers to Rahab's house. Here the story focuses on her and is filled with the drama of her hiding of the spies, lying to the king's men, sending the soldiers off on a wild goose chase, and assisting the spies as they escaped over the wall.

We are simply told that the spies "came to the house of a harlot named Rahab and lodged there" (v. 1). The word *lodged* is a general one meaning to "lie down." Although it can indicate sexual intercourse, it is more commonly used for assuming a prone position for sleeping. Some critics interpret that their action was carnal and insist that the spies were taking advantage of Rahab's profession, but the Scripture gives no indication that their motives or actions were anything of the sort. It is possible that Rahab was no longer practicing her profession when the spies came to her house. Consider two reasons. First the spies found that she had believed in Israel's God before they arrived. Second, the piles of flax on her roof, under which she hid them, may indicate that she had changed her profession to making garments. Apart from using it for her profession, Rahab's "house" was probably somewhat similar to a tavern where men gathered and talked. As such, it was an ideal place for the spies, coming as visitors, to enter unobtrusively, find accommodation, and hopefully obtain the information they wanted from other patrons. Apparently, Rahab ascertained who the spies were and was sympathetic to them. She would have known that they had been reported to the king, and she recognized the need for quick action.

Rahab Lies to the King's Men (vv. 3-7)

Rahab had already hidden the spies on the roof when the king's men arrived at her door demanding that they be brought out (v. 3). The flat roofs of ancient houses were used for many purposes, including the drying of flax. She had carefully piled stalks of flax over the men so that they would not be seen. In response to the king's police demand for the men, she replied, "Yes, the men came to me, but I did not know where they were from. And it happened as the gate was being shut, when it was dark, the men went out. Where the men went I do not know; pursue them quickly, for you may overtake them" (vv. 4-5).

Rahab's Ethics

Although Rahab's patriotic responsibility was to turn the men over to the king, she did not do that. Instead, she hid them. As a citizen of Jericho, therefore, she was guilty of treason. Not only were her actions and speech deceptive, but she told several direct lies to the king's soldiers. Rahab's lying has understandably raised a number of questions. The ninth commandment specifically addresses this sin, and lying is roundly condemned in the book of Proverbs as well as generally throughout Scripture. The ethics of what Rahab said present a conundrum which people are free to discuss and debate. We should observe, however, that the Bible never *commends* Rahab for lying; the biblical account simply records what she did, as a historical fact.

For Rahab, her choice was clear. It was her moral obligation to protect the two men whose cause and God she now firmly believed in. Her allegiance to the city of Jericho stood in direct conflict to her faithfulness to Israel's God and to the spies as His representatives. Because she now considered herself to be a subject of Israel, she acted on Israel's behalf.

Rahab's Faith

It is Rahab's faith, not her profession, or her lying, which shines in this chapter. Religiously, she was a pagan Canaanite woman who deserved the judgment of God. Morally, she is identified with her sinful life as "Rahab the harlot" in almost every mention of her name in the Bible.

Rahab acted on the information she received about the one true God, and as a result she was delivered from the judgment God brought on Jericho, which pictures His condemnation on all sin. In the New Testament, Rahab's faith is commended: "By faith the harlot Rahab did not perish with those who did not believe, when she had received the spies with peace" (Heb. 11:31). James mentions the same thing when he says, "Likewise, was not Rahab the harlot also justified by works when she received the messengers and sent them out another way?" (James 2:25). When Rahab welcomed the spies, trusting her and her family's welfare into their hands, she outwardly demonstrated her inward belief in Israel's God; it was faith in action.

Rahab Explains her Faith (vv. 8-9)

With the king's men off searching for the spies along the road to the Jordan, Rahab had a chance to talk to the spies on the roof where they still lay hidden. The first thing she said to them was that she knew that Yahweh, the covenant keeping God, had given them the land (v. 9). What a statement of faith! Then she confided to them about how the people of Jericho were reacting to the presence of the Israelites and to their understanding of Israel's God. They knew that Yahweh had dried up a path through the Red Sea after the children of Israel left Egypt. They had heard what had happened to the two kings of the Amorites, Sihon and Og, only a few months earlier (Num. 21:21-35). She specifically mentioned that Israel had "utterly destroyed" the Amorite armies (v. 10; Deut. 10:17).

Rahab believed her city was doomed when she heard what the Lord had done for the Israelites. In spanning the forty years from the time of the Red Sea crossing to the victory over the Amorites, she reasoned that if Yahweh had defeated enemies as strong as the Egyptians and the Amorites (and had obviously cared for the Israelites in the meantime), He would certainly have no trouble defeating the Canaanites. Her reasoning led her to put her faith in Israel's God. Unlike Rahab, the people of Jericho's knowledge was not "mixed with faith" (cf. Heb. 4:2); their "reasoning" led them to have such paralyzing fear that they sought to destroy the spies who represented Israel. Moses had predicted this fear just after they crossed the Red Sea. In his song he said, "All the inhabitants of Canaan will melt away. Fear and dread will fall on them; by the greatness of Your arm they will be as still as stone" (Ex. 15:15-16).

Rahab's Song

Perhaps Rahab's most remarkable statement is at the end of verse 11: "For the LORD your God, He is God in heaven above and on earth beneath." According to this statement she believed Israel's God to be above the gods of Canaan. She also believed Him to be the only God, for she said "He is God." And she believed Him to be the sovereign Lord, ruler of both heaven and earth. The strong implication is that, because she believed that He could save the Israelites, He could also save those Gentiles who came to Him.

Rahab's confession is sometimes called the "Song of Rahab." The song indicates that her whole personality—her intellect, her emotions, and her will—were all involved in her response to Israel's God. What she "knew" involved her intellect, as she understood that Jehovah was the one true God. Her faith was based on facts. What she "feared" involved her emotions. She was afraid of coming judgment for herself and her family when she heard of God's acting on Israel's behalf. What she "did" in receiving the spies was an act of the will as she pleaded for the salvation of herself and her family.

Rahab's response pictures how people are truly saved today. They learn from Scripture of the way of salvation. They fear God's judgment on sin, and they repent. Finally, they willfully acknowledge that God's condemnation is righteous and they accept the salvation provided through the sacrifice of His Son, the Lord Jesus Christ.

Rahab Makes a Request (vv. 12-13)

Rahab requested that the spies swear to her by the name of the Yahweh, "since I have shown you kindness, that you also will show kindness to my father's house." It would be an oath of protection. The word "kindness" is a word sometimes translated "love" in the Psalms and means "a reciprocal relationship of caring." Rahab had shown kindness to the spies. Now she expected kindness from them for her entire family. She had an immediate concern for her loved ones. Rahab may have expected nothing more than that the Israelites would take them alive as prisoners. We know from the Bible's account that Rahab's family was not only spared death in the conquest of Jericho but were assimilated into the national life of Israel (6:25). Rahab's family demonstrated their own faith by gathering in her house when the Israelites later surrounded the city.

Some commentators think that the spies' conversation with Rahab violated the commands of God not to have any dealings or make any agreements with the Canaanites at all (cf. Deut. 7:1-5, 20:16-18). However, the story is not about Rahab the pagan Canaanite, but about Rahab the newly converted Canaanite who had switched allegiance to the one true God. In effect she was now an Israelite in her heart.

The Spies Escape From Jericho (vv. 14–20)

The spies promised to "deal kindly and truly" with her family when the time came to destroy Jericho, but the promise was on condition that none of the family divulged the fact that the spies had been there (v. 14). Thus, the agreement was made for the protection of the spies in the near term and for the protection of Rahab's family in the longer term. The words "kindly and truly" used by the spies were a foretaste of the "grace and truth" that would eventually come through the Lord Jesus Christ (cf. John 1:17). This idea is conveyed by Old Testament writers in the words "mercy and truth" or "loving-kindness and truth" and usually foreshadows the grace of the Lord Jesus in balance with the justice of a holy God. Both loving-kindness and truth met at the cross in accomplishing our justification (Rom. 3:21-26).

Rahab then helped them escape by letting them down by a rope through a window, "for her house was on the city wall" (v. 15). The location of her house should not surprise us: the remains of ancient houses built on the old city wall of Jericho have been discovered by archeologists. Rahab shrewdly advised the spies to go west up into the hills to escape, rather than east toward the Jordan, which was the direction in which she had sent the pursuers. She instructed them to hide there for three days (v. 16). The men answered that they would be absolved of the oath they had sworn to save her and her family unless she met two conditions. First, she needed to "bind this line of scarlet cord in the window through which you have let us down" (v. 18). They could identify her house accurately if the red cord was displayed (maybe hanging down slightly, since the authorities would not have allowed her to hang a cord from her window to the ground with the prospect of being under siege). It was probably not the same rope by which she let down the spies. A different Hebrew word is used for the "cord" in verse 18 from the word "rope" in verse 15. The red cord would be the special sign to the Israelites.

The second condition was that if her family were to be saved, they needed to be with her in her house at the time. The spies solemnly swore that if anyone was not in her house, his blood would be on his head, and that if the family was in her house, "his blood," or the guilt of bloodshed, would be on their heads if a hand was laid on them (vv. 18-19). For her family to gather there in her house, they would have had to believe that Jericho was going to fall, that Israel's God was stronger than their Canaanite idols, and that they could safely commit themselves to the Israelites when they captured the city. In other words, like Rahab, they had to be believers in Israel's God.

The Red Cord (v. 21)

Although this conversation between Rahab and the spies occurred after the record of her letting them down from the wall (vv. 15-20), it likely took place while they were still in Rahab's house. We can hardly imagine that the spies were shouting from the ground to Rahab in the window on the top of the wall in the middle of the night at a time of high tension! Neither they nor Rahab wanted to be discovered in that situation. After the spies departed, Rahab bound the scarlet cord in the window.

The red cord has been viewed as a symbol of the blood of Christ by many Christians since the time of Clement of Rome. What we can definitely say is that it was a mark of identification and a sign of safety from judgment. A remarkable similarity is seen in the blood sprinkled on the lintel and doorposts of the Israelites' houses in Egypt before the exodus (Exodus 12), as the blood of the Passover was also a mark of safety from judgment. In both cases, safety was only possible if they stayed in their homes (v. 19; Ex. 12:22), and it was God who spared those who, in faith, followed His instructions.

The Spies Return (vv. 22-24)

After the spies departed Jericho, they traveled up into the hills and stayed there for three days until the pursuers had given up the chase. It is not necessary to think of the three days as full twenty-four-hour days. The term "three days" often indicates parts of three days. The spies had left Shittim and talked to Rahab the first day. They hid that night and all the next day. Sometime during the third day they returned to their camp. When they did return, "They came to Joshua . . . and told him all that had befallen them."

Their report was positive: "Truly the LORD has delivered all the land into our hands, for indeed all the inhabitants of the country are fainthearted because of us." This statement was probably the essential part of a longer message, because they told him "all that had befallen them." Their words were similar to Rahab's words when she had first talked to them (v. 9). Instead of strategic military information, it was spiritual encouragement observing how God had prepared their enemies for the takeover. God had been faithful to His promise, and the inhabitants of Jericho were shaking with fear.

In Conclusion

It is interesting to compare the report of the two spies with the report of the ten spies thirty-eight years earlier. Both teams saw the same things, but these two special agents saw the situation in light of God's promises and they concluded that God had already given Israel the entire land, not just Jericho. We should all look through the lens of God's promises when challenging situations develop in our own lives and take hold of the spiritual blessings God has promised us as Christians.

Several evidences of Rahab's faith emerge in this chapter. First, she defied the authority of the king of Jericho and announced her belief in Israel's God, putting her life in jeopardy as far as Jericho authorities was concerned, but securing her life as far as God was concerned. Second, she identified herself with God's people when she bound the red cord in her window. Third, she was concerned for the salvation of her relatives. God honored Rehab by giving her a place in the ancestry of the Lord Jesus Christ (Matt. 1:5).

Joshua 3

The Crossing of the Jordan

The River Jordan was the last barrier between the Israelites and the Promised Land. This chapter chronicles the crossing of the river. It was the single most significant event since the exodus from Egypt and the giving of the Law to Moses on Mount Sinai. It was, essentially, the culmination of the prophetic revelations that God gave to Abraham, Isaac, and Jacob successively many hundreds of years earlier.

The River Jordan

Today the Jordan is a small river; most of it is drawn off for irrigation and domestic use. Even in Bible times it was not considered sizeable, measuring only about one hundred feet wide and from three to ten feet deep. At springtime, however, floods from rains and the melting snows of Mount Hermon caused it to run much deeper, faster, and wider, creating a span between the banks of anything up to *six* hundred feet. For a mass movement of two million people with large herds of domestic animals, it presented a formidable obstacle. Just as the Red Sea had hindered God's people from leaving Egypt, so the Jordan River hindered them from entering Canaan. Most of this generation would have been too young to remember the Red Sea crossing, as all the adult generation at that time had died in the wilderness, with the exception of Joshua and Caleb. The new generation needed to learn the lesson of trusting God to overcome a seemingly impossible barrier.

Many details are given about this remarkable event. They show the importance of this crossing in God's plan for His people. Notice the careful preparations and buildup to the crossing:

- ➢ Gathering provisions
- ➢ Sanctifying themselves spiritually before God
- ➢ Carefully arranging the order of their advance in relation to the ark of the covenant and the priests carrying it
- ➢ The crossing itself
- ➢ Setting the two sets of memorial stones

All these steps were to firmly impress on the people the significance of the event, that God was giving them the land and was acting powerfully to bring them into it. As difficulties arose later in their campaign to capture Canaan, they could recall how God opened the way for them to cross the Jordan and, in so doing, renew their courage and finish their task.

The Red Sea and the River Jordan

The crossing of the Jordan can be contrasted to and compared with the crossing of the Red Sea in the many complementary lessons they teach believers about the Christian experience:

- In crossing the Red Sea, Israel was separated from Egypt. This speaks of our separation from the world, which is now *behind* us. In crossing the Jordan they were entering the Promised Land which lay *before* them, speaking of the breadth and provisions of the new life we experience when we follow Christ (cf. John 10:9-10).
- Crossing the Red Sea symbolizes Christ's conquering sin's power over us in His resurrection, as pictured by the armies of Pharaoh that were drowned by a *one-time* powerful act of God. Crossing the Jordan speaks of the *ongoing* good fight of faith in which *we* must engage in order to enjoy the blessings God has for us, just as Israel had to meet, engage, and defeat the Canaanite city states one by one.
- Crossing the Red Sea introduced them to *defensive* warfare against the wilderness peoples. The enemies who attacked them needed to be repulsed, so they could move on. Crossing the Jordan introduced them to *offensive* warfare against the Canaanites, who needed to be defeated and destroyed.
- In crossing the Red Sea, the children of Israel committed themselves to *Moses' leadership*. As the New Testament puts it, they were "baptized into Moses" (1 Cor. 10:2). In crossing the Jordan, they submitted to *Joshua's leadership*. Believers today are to be committed to the Lord Jesus Christ, who is greater than both Moses and Joshua.

Many believers today are quite happy to escape the judgment of God in Egypt as depicted by the destroying Angel, but they shy away from fighting the battles that give entrance into the land of victory and blessing. They fear the dangers and discomforts of spiritual warfare. Consequently, they get no further in their Christian experience than the banks of the Jordan and seldom, if ever, enjoy the blessing of victorious Christian living. The central lessons are the necessity to trust and obey.

Three Days (vv. 1-2)

In the first section of this chapter, Joshua prepared the people to move and then led them from Shittim (Acacia Grove) to a campsite perhaps ten miles from the east bank of Jordan. They had been encamped in Shittim for months, ever since their victory over the two Amorite kings, Sihon and Og. They had completed a three-day preparation period during the final days in Shittim and would spend another three days on the banks of the Jordan before crossing over (v. 2; 1:11).

The two three-day periods are different as to (1) when Joshua spoke to the people, (2) what he told them to do, and (3) location. On Day 1 of the first period, the people were in Shittim and the officers were told by Joshua to instruct the people to prepare provisions (1:11). Then on Day 3, "Joshua rose early . . . and came to the Jordan . . . and lodged there" (3:1). However, in the second period, it was on Day 3, when they had been three days lodging on the banks of the Jordan, that Joshua himself instructed the people of what to do when they saw the ark (vv. 2-3).

The Ark of the Covenant (v. 3)

Joshua announced on the third day, "When you see the ark of the covenant of the LORD your God and the priests, the Levites, bearing it, then you shall set out from your place and go after it." This is the first mention of the ark in Joshua. It becomes a most significant feature of the book, mentioned some thirty times all together and nine times in this chapter alone. The ark is the central feature of the crossing of the Jordan, and it is important that we understand why.

The ark of the covenant was constructed by the Israelites thirty-eight years earlier while they were encamped at Mount Sinai. It was the most sacred piece of furniture in the tabernacle, being the sole piece to occupy the Most Holy Place. It was not their invention, but built according to God's specific instructions as to its shape, dimensions, and materials. It was a chest-shaped box made of acacia wood and sheathed with gold both inside and out with a solid gold lid called the mercy seat. On the lid stood two figures of angels (called cherubim) which faced each other. Their wings were spread forward and touched the wings of the other while they looked down at the mercy seat. Inside the ark were the two tables of the Law. Once a year, on the Day of Atonement, the high priest would enter the Most Holy Place and sprinkle the blood of the atonement on the golden mercy seat.

What the Ark Symbolizes

The ark of the covenant was highly symbolic. The wood in its construction represented the humanity of the Lord Jesus Christ, while the gold spoke of His deity. The Law of God within it spoke of God's righteous standards which were fully met by Christ in His spotless character. Man had hopelessly failed to meet those standards and was, therefore, under condemnation. However, between sinful man and the holy Law of God was the blood-sprinkled mercy seat. The blood symbolized man's sin being atoned, or covered, and God's righteous demands being propitiated, satisfied, and appeased (Rom. 3:25). God was demonstrating that the only basis for a relationship between man and God was through the person and work of the coming Redeemer. As the God/Man, Jesus Christ would satisfy an offended God and atone for man's sin.

The ark was not a cultic object which, if worshipped, would bring good fortune to God's people. To the Israelites the ark symbolized the covenant that God had made with His people and His presence with them. They could not see God, but this visible symbol reminded them that He was with them. Just as Christ was the visible presence of God among the people in His day (John 1:14), so the ark was the visible presence of God among His people in the Old Testament. The people never actually saw the ark itself as it was either housed in the Most Holy Place in the tabernacle when they were encamped or draped when in transit. Numbers 4:5-6 records God's instructions as to how the ark was to be transported: it was to be covered with several layers of materials: first, the veil of the tabernacle, then badgers skin, then a blue cloth.

However, in symbolizing God's presence, the ark was to be the focus of the Israelites' attention. When they looked at it, they would remember the solemn covenant God had made with them, which included the promise that the land into which they were entering would be theirs. Thus, they were to keep their eyes on the ark. The Christian believer today needs to keep his eyes (the eyes of faith) on the person and the work of the Lord Jesus Christ so that He can lead us into the place of blessing and victory. The Israelites were told to wait until they saw the ark, and only then were they to "set out . . . and go after it."

The Space between the Ark and the People (v. 4)

The people were told not to come near the ark but to preserve a distance of two thousand cubits (ca. one thousand yards) between it and them. This request was similar to God's command to the people concerning Mount Sinai: "Set bounds for the people all around, saying 'Take heed to yourselves that you do not go up the mountain or touch its base'" (Ex. 19:12). The gap demonstrated a reverential respect and awe for the majesty, holiness, and greatness of God. It carries the idea of the fear of the Lord, which is a regular theme throughout the Bible. In our day, some Christians tend to have a casual attitude toward approaching God and His Son. When we truly appreciate God's glory we will pay Him the respect that He deserves.

This separation also gave all the people an uninterrupted view of the ark. The large numbers of people were to directly follow this symbol of God's covenant and presence rather than simply the person in front of them. Each person could be assured that he or she was on track if they kept their eyes on the ark. We too are to individually keep our spiritual eyes on the Lord Jesus

Christ, who is pictured so clearly in the ark: not following one another, but together following Him who is the Pioneer (Author) and Perfecter (Finisher) of faith (Heb. 12:2). The word to the people from Joshua's officers continued, "Do not come near it, that you may know the way by which you must go, for you have not passed this way before." As the ark went before the Israelites, the Lord went before His people into the land of blessing and victory. We might miss the way if we do not follow Him of whom the ark speaks. He who triumphed over all *His* foes calls us to follow Him (Col. 2:15).

Consecration to Christ (v. 5)

At this point, Joshua himself spoke to all the people about their need to consecrate themselves to the Lord. "Sanctify yourselves, for tomorrow the LORD will do wonders among you." The word, *sanctify* means to "set apart" for God, to "be holy and clean." The basic idea involves separation from anything unclean, anything that would contaminate the purity of a relationship with God. Since God is holy, His people must be separated from anything inconsistent with His holiness. Their sanctification was a necessary prerequisite for crossing over to the land of victory and blessing. Before the Lord gave the Law on Mount Sinai, God told Moses to sanctify the people (Ex. 19:10, 14, 15). They had to ceremonially wash their clothes and refrain from marital intimacy to prepare for that significant event. So it was now for the Israelites on the banks of the Jordan, for, as Joshua said, "Tomorrow the LORD will do wonders among you."

Spiritual cleansing is a solid New Testament truth. The New Testament calls on all believers to be holy, or sanctified (see 2 Cor. 7:1 and 1 Peter 1:16; 3:15). We need to continually confess our sins. When we do that, "He is faithful . . . to cleanse us from all unrighteousness" (1 John 1:9). We are also urged to dedicate ourselves wholly to the Lord (Rom. 12:1).

The Command to the Priests (v. 6)

Although Joshua did not give instructions to the people till the third day, it appears that the purpose for their having three days on the banks of Jordan was to prepare emotionally and spiritually to take the next important step in their progress toward inheriting the land. They needed to be forcibly impressed with the state of the flooded river so that they could understand the extent of the miracle God was about to do in bringing them across it. They needed time to reflect on God's ways and to rededicate themselves to Him.

Joshua turned from speaking to the people to speak to the priests. To them he said, "Take up the ark of the covenant and cross over before the people." The order of the story at this point is more thematic in nature than chronological. Verse 5 ends the description of the three-day stay on the banks of the Jordan. The command to take up the ark in verse 6 actually took place on the morning of the next day, the day on which Israel crossed the Jordan. Chronologically it belongs between verses 13 and 14. However, the theme of taking up the ark is introduced here because, symbolically, the ark going before them was an important aspect of this great event in Israel's history. Without the ark, none of the events that followed would have meaning.

Joshua's Leadership is Recognized (vv. 7-8)

The day dawned for crossing the Jordan. In the events of the past six days, Joshua had done nothing spectacular. He possessed no special rod like the one Moses had used to such dramatic effect in the exodus and the wilderness journey. Yet despite the fact that Joshua would do no special feat in the crossing of the Jordan either, God said to him, "This day I will begin to magnify you in the sight of all Israel, that they may know that as I was with Moses, so I will be with you." God would exalt him, and he would be honored after this special day. God would do it, and no one could accuse Joshua of exalting himself.

In the minds of the people, Joshua would now assume Moses' place with Moses' authority. The people would know with certainty that God was with him, even as He had promised (1:9). When God gives obedient men honor and authority, the results bring glory to God and blessing to His people. Joshua had not sought the honor; God gave it to him. When men seek honor and authority for selfish reasons, however, it spells trouble for both the people they lead and the decisions they make. We should be aware of this danger.

God told Joshua to command the priests bearing the ark that, when they came to the water's edge, they were to stand there. With everyone looking intently at the ark, they listened closely for what Joshua would say next. It was a dramatic moment.

Joshua Commands the People to Listen to the Living God (vv. 9-10)

With emphasis on the moment, the passage then says, "So Joshua said to the children of Israel, Come here and hear the words of the LORD your God." This is the third command of Joshua to the people. Six days earlier, when they were in Shittim, he had told them through his officers to "prepare provisions" (1:11). On the previous day he had said, "Sanctify yourselves" (3:5). Clearly, God had already revealed to him what would happen and he now wanted them to listen to God's words, not his own. He was truly a *spiritual* leader.

Joshua then said, "By this you shall know." What "this" refers to is what God was about to do in rolling back the floodwaters. The Israelites were understandably fearful of the swollen river, but when they saw the miracle they would come to know that the "living God" (in contrast to the lifeless gods of the Canaanites which would be revealed as powerless) was among them. He would, "without fail," drive out their enemies as they possessed the land. They would experience both God's presence and God's power.

The list of the seven peoples in Canaan mentioned in verse 10 contained the names of the seven primary people groups in Canaan at the time. Five such lists occur in Joshua (3:10; 9:1; 11:3; 12:8; 24:11), and a total of twenty-three lists are found in the Old Testament. In the combined lists, twelve separate peoples are named, but the seven listed here seem to be the main ones. The name "Canaanites" is used sometimes to refer to all the peoples in the land. At other times, as in this passage, it refers to the specific ethnic tribes living both along the coast and near the Jordan (cf. Num. 13:29). Other than those specifically called Canaanites, five of the groups were peoples descended from the sons of Canaan (the son of Ham): the Hittites, the Girgashites, the Hivites, the Jebusites, and the Amorites (Gen. 10:15-17). Little is known of the Perizzites, but all seven were pagan peoples whose cup of iniquity was now full; they were ripe for God's judgment (cf. Gen. 15:16).

"Behold, the ark" (v. 11)

With all the Israelites in a semi-circle around the ark and keeping a distance of at least one thousand yards, Joshua began to speak. Presumably, criers repeated his words so that all would hear. Joshua focused the attention of the surrounding multitude on the ark. The priests carrying it were standing at the edge of the river. He shouted, "Behold, the ark of the covenant of the Lord of all the earth is crossing over before you into the Jordan." He captured their attention with the word "behold." The ark stood not only for Israel's God but the "living God" (v. 10); He is greater than the gods of the pagan nations, which have external form but no life (Ps. 115:4-7). Even more than that, the ark stood for "the Lord of all the earth," the sovereign God who can do whatever He wishes anywhere, at any time, in any way.

Twelve Men (v. 12)

Joshua then called twelve men, one man from each tribe. The same words will be used again in chapter 4. The reason it is mentioned here seems to be part of Joshua's plan to build the story slowly toward a climax. Themes are introduced, only to be repeated later as a device to increase the reader's anticipation. This literary device was used earlier in this chapter with the mention of the priests in verse 3, telling them what they were to do in verse 8, and adding to the instruction in verse 13. The selection of the twelve men here in verse 12 will appear again when we will learn what they, as representatives of the twelve tribes, were required to do (4:2).

"The waters . . . shall stand as a heap" (v. 13)

At last we learn what the "wonders" were that God would actually do (cf. v. 5). Joshua announced, "And it shall come to pass that as soon as the soles of the feet of the priests who bear the ark of the LORD, the Lord of all the earth, shall rest in the waters of the Jordan, that the waters of the Jordan shall be cut off, the waters that come down from upstream, and they shall stand as a heap." God was going to stop the floodwaters upstream so that they could all cross over through the bed of the river. "The LORD, the Lord of all the earth" would accomplish this. As the "LORD" (Yahweh), He would keep His covenant with them. As "Lord [Adonai, meaning master] of all the earth," He had the right to take over the land of Canaan.

The Crossing of Jordan (vv. 14-17)

It must have been an awesome sight. Two million people with all their possessions and livestock stood in a huge semi-circle. The multitude touched the river at both ends on the north and on the south. A space of more than half a mile separated them all from the four priests in the center carrying the ark of the covenant and standing at the edge of the flooded river. The priests were not touching the ark itself but, in accordance with the Law (Num. 4:15), were carrying it by means of two poles threaded through the rings on the sides of the ark. Every eye must have been riveted on the scene. Then, in one dramatic moment, the priests stepped forward in faith and obedience and entered the swirling floodwater. At that moment the miracle happened.

The floodwaters receded and the water level suddenly dropped. We are not told how long it took, but soon all the water drained away and nothing but the empty riverbed separated them from the land of Canaan. The river was stopped up. The barrier was gone. What happened to the water of the river is simply described in these words: "The waters which came down from upstream stood still, and rose in a heap very far away at Adam, the city that is beside Zeretan. So the waters that went down into the Sea of Arabah, the Salt Sea, failed, and were cut off; and the people crossed over opposite Jericho" (v. 16). Adam is thought to be about twenty miles upstream from the crossing point. The Sea of Arabah is the Dead Sea.

Five hundred years later the psalmist composed a song about the rolling back of the Jordan for all to sing: "The sea saw it and fled; Jordan turned back. The mountains skipped like rams, the little hills like lambs. What ails you, O sea, that you fled? O Jordan that you turned back? O mountains, that you skipped like rams? O little hills like lambs?" (Ps. 114:3-6). Is there a natural explanation for it? Does the poetic language of the psalmist indicate that an earthquake had occurred? Whatever happened, it was God who caused it at precisely the right moment when the feet of the priests touched the water. It was a miracle of huge proportions.

The Ark in the Middle of the River (v. 17)

When the priests carrying the ark reached the middle of the dry bed of the Jordan, they "stood firm." It is the same word used of the waters in the previous verse where it is stated that they "stood still." The ark remained stationary in the middle of the river during the entire time that it took the people to cross over. Note the double reference to the *dry* ground on which the priests stood firm and the people walked over. There were no pools of water to avoid, nor was the river bed muddy and soft. The bed of the Red Sea that they had crossed forty years before was also referred to as "dry ground" (Neh. 9:11; cf. Ex. 9:11). When God performs a mighty miracle, He does it thoroughly.

An Allegory for Believers

The whole scene of the Israelites crossing the Jordan is highly instructive to believers. It is another feature in the history of Israel that pictures the Christian experience. The Israelites had been redeemed by the blood of the Passover lamb in Egypt, which pictures our redemption by the blood of Christ. They had been delivered from the bondage of Egypt and from the power of Pharaoh when they crossed the Red Sea, just as the believer has been delivered from the bondage of sin and the power of Satan by Christ's death on the cross and victorious resurrection. They had been nurtured in the wilderness by the provisions that God had supplied such as manna, water, guidance, and protection. So too, God supplies the needs of His people in their journey through the wilderness of this world.

Now, in the crossing of the Jordan, the Israelites were leaving the wilderness and entering into the privileges and blessings of the inheritance God had given them. For them, their inheritance was material: built-up cities, established farms, and fertile land. But it was still occupied with enemies that had to be overcome. They were entering the land by faith. All this pictures the believer claiming the spiritual promises God has given us—our present spiritual inheritance—that we can enjoy now, before we get to heaven. There are spiritual enemies to be overcome, but there are victories and blessings to be enjoyed.

In Conclusion

Crossing the Jordan pictures several important keys to entering this new level of Christian living. First, Joshua, their leader would be exalted (v. 7). He pictures the risen Christ whom God has highly exalted (Phil. 2:9). The growing believer will want to exalt Christ in everything he or she says and does. Second, Joshua would lead them to victory in their battles, just as the Captain of our salvation, the Lord Jesus Christ, leads us to "triumph" over our spiritual enemies (2 Cor. 2:14). Third, the ark, which was a picture of God's powerful presence among them, was to be the focus of all the people (v. 3). They were not to move until the ark moved. Likewise, when believers keep their eyes on the Lord Jesus and follow Him, they can be sure they are on the right path leading to the land of blessing.

Joshua 4

The Memorial Stones

In chapter 3 Joshua describes how the Israelites crossed the River Jordan. The Canaanites in Jericho, meanwhile, were undoubtedly watching the whole drama intently from a distance, for the Israelites were essentially invading their land. From what Rahab said, we know that the reports of how God had acted on behalf of His people on the other side of the Jordan had left them paralyzed with fear (2:10). In normal circumstances their army would have tried to defend the country at the river, which was a vulnerable point (particularly during the annual flood) for any army trying to cross. But Jericho's army did nothing, even though it was a mere five miles away. As Rahab told the spies, "Our hearts melted; neither did there remain any more courage in any one" (2:11). She, however, was quietly waiting with her family in her house to be delivered.

Twelve Men and Twelve Stones (vv. 1-3)

Chapter 4 begins with the Israelites having nearly completed crossing the Jordan. The priests were still at their station in the middle of the riverbed, bearing the ark. At this point God told Joshua to oversee the building of a ceremonial pillar of stones, on the west (Canaan) bank of the river. After doing so he built another in the place where the ark had stood all day while the people crossed over. The stone pillars were to be memorials of what had happened that day.

God told Joshua to select twelve men, one man from each tribe, as representatives of all the people. Joshua had already given this same directive (3:12). The apparent difficulty of this command being given twice is dispelled when we understand the literary device Joshua was using which first mentions an activity then later adds more details about it in a second mention. It appears that God had previously told him what the twelve were to do (3:12) and now the time had come to actually do it (4:2-3). After collecting the stones the men were to "leave them" at their "place of lodging" that night. The phrase "leave them" is an uncommon expression meaning "cause them to rest." This expression may have been connected in the author's mind with the "rest" that the Israelites would find in Canaan, which is one of the themes of Joshua (1:13, 15, 3:13 etc.).

Joshua's Command (vv. 4-7)

After God had commanded Joshua, he in turn called and commanded the twelve men, telling them to "cross over before the ark of the LORD your God in the midst of Jordan" (v. 4). The place where they were to get the stones is described carefully as the *middle of Jordan*, "before the ark," or "in the presence of the ark." The ark is central to every activity in this chapter. Note also that the ark is called the "ark of the LORD," God's covenant name. Each of the twelve was to find a stone right there and carry it back to the camp on his shoulder. The twelve men represented the tribes of Israel as a unified people. The unifying factor was the ark, and the stones taken from where it stood were associated with the ark.

"When your children ask . . ."

The stones taken from where the ark stood were to be a sign to the coming generations of Israelites. When their children asked, "What do these stones mean to you?" the older generation was to answer, "The waters of the Jordan were cut off before the ark of the covenant of the LORD; when it crossed over the Jordan, the waters of the Jordan were cut off" (v. 7). They were to tell them that God had worked an outstanding miracle in stopping the floodwaters of the river because the ark, representing God's power and presence, was there.

The idea of parents educating their children with a memorial about the wonderful works and ways of God is something God had used before with the Israelites. When their children asked about the Passover, they were to answer, "It is the Passover sacrifice of the LORD who passed over the houses of the children of Israel" (Ex. 12:26-27). When their children asked about the practice of redeeming the firstborn son or male domestic animal with a sacrificed lamb they were to answer, "By strength of hand the LORD brought us out of Egypt" when He killed all the firstborn of Egypt (Ex. 13:14-16). Parents were also to have an answer when their children asked about the ceremonial laws given to them (Deut. 6:20-24). Today, Christian parents should have clear answers for their children when they ask about Christian practices such as baptism or the Lord's Supper.

The Ark Opened the Way

When the twelve men made a pillar with the stones on the west bank, Joshua states that "the children of Israel did so" (v. 8). The twelve men represented the people in obeying the command of Joshua to the letter, "as the LORD had spoken to Joshua." When they saw the pillar of stones they were always to remember that the basis of their being in Canaan was that the ark had opened the way through a formidable barrier.

The Ark Conquered Death

The stones were made into a pillar on the west bank of the Jordan to be a visible "memorial to the children of Israel forever" (v. 7), and especially during the campaign of conquering Canaan. They would remember that Yahweh their God was present with them and had worked wonders for them; that the ark had stood in the place of death while they entered into the land of promise and blessing. They would learn to "tremble . . . at the presence of the God of Jacob" (Ps. 114:7). Symbolically the ark had conquered death. The blood on the mercy seat of the ark standing in the riverbed pictures for us the Lord Jesus Christ who went down into the place of death to allow His people to enter into the riches of their inheritance in Him.

In addition to the lesson that the ark conquered death, the pillar of stones on the banks of the Jordan taught the Israelites another important lesson. Their feet now stood on the land of their inheritance. The stones witnessed to the fact that both the ark and the people had been brought from the place of death to the place of resurrection. It symbolizes for us the wonderful New Testament truth that believers are risen with Christ to walk in newness of life (Rom. 6:4-5; Col. 3:1).

Twelve Stones in the Midst of Jordan (v. 9)

We now read that Joshua built another memorial pillar of stones—this one, in the middle of the Jordan, where the ark had been. Though we do not read that God specifically commanded Joshua to erect these stones, his memorializing of that place should not be surprising. The pillar of stones was still there "till this day," the day of writing. It would probably have been visible when the water of the Jordan was low during the dry season.

This second set of twelve stones is only mentioned in this verse. Not all scholars are agreed that it speaks of a second set of stones. The New International Version takes the view that there was only one pillar by adding two words that are not in the original Hebrew. It reads that the twelve stones *had been* in the Jordan and were, therefore, the same stones made into a pillar on the west bank. However, our text reflects the original Hebrew, which clearly says, "Joshua set up twelve stones in the midst of the Jordan." It implies that these were twelve *different* stones than the ones carried to the western bank of the river. They were set up in a different place—in the middle of Jordan. A different person—Joshua himself—set them up. And, as signs, they teach a different lesson.

Joshua's Pillar of Thanksgiving (v. 9)

The first pillar was built by the twelve men representing the people of Israel who had been brought from the place of death and were now on the resurrection side, the place of new life and blessing. The second pillar was erected by Joshua. He built it in the middle of the river where the ark had been, protecting all Israel from the floodwaters. He built it in thankfulness to God as a memorial of what God had done for him and his people. It stood as a memorial to the bloodstained mercy seat (the symbol of atonement for sin) which had remained there until the last Israelites had passed over.

This day was the one on which God had promised He would exalt Joshua in the eyes of the people (3:7). And, faithful to His word, He did exalt him that day (4:14). But Joshua never wanted to forget that the basis of his exaltation and leadership was not in his own abilities: it was based in what God had done for him and for the Israelites. For the rest of his life, as he was leading the Israelites from one victory to another in Canaan, he would remember the pile of stones he had built in the Jordan and what it signified of the saving power of God.

Remembering Christ's Finished Work

For believers today a significant application may be gained from Joshua's pillar in the middle of the Jordan: we are never to forget the finished work of Christ on the cross as pictured by the ark, with its blood-sprinkled mercy seat, in the place of death. Though we have been raised with Christ to resurrection life and have been given blessing after blessing from the inexhaustible riches of His grace, we are to constantly return to the source of it all in His work on the cross. For this reason the Lord Jesus Christ instituted the remembrance feast. Of each symbol He said, "Do this in remembrance of me." The apostle Paul observed: "As often as you eat this bread and drink this cup, you proclaim the Lord's death till He comes" (1 Cor. 11:24-26). It is for this reason also that the cross has become the symbol of Christianity.

The Centrality of the Ark (vv. 10-11)

After building the two stone memorials the story of Joshua returns to the details of the crossing (vv. 10-11). Once again the emphasis is placed on the ark that the priests bore on their shoulders in the middle of the riverbed, "until everything was finished." He also reminds us also that there was a chain of command. God first commanded Moses, then Moses commanded Joshua, and Joshua commanded the people (v. 10; cf. Deut. 31:7, Josh. 1:1-2, 10-11). All three of them had followed their instructions to the letter. We read then that, "The people hurried and crossed over" (v. 10). Obviously they had a limited time to complete the crossing before the waters returned, so they hurried. True obedience is not obedience unless it is immediate and complete.

Finally, when they had all crossed over, the priests who had been bearing the ark the entire day carried it out of the river bed to the new camp on the west side of the Jordan. They did this in the "presence of," or in sight of, all the people. When the priests carrying it first stepped into the river and the waters dried up, all Israel saw what happened. From the beginning of that long day until the end, the ark was the center of everyone's attention, just as God planned it. A good application for Christians who want to move from their half-hearted "wilderness experience" to the possession of their spiritual inheritance may be found here. The key is to keep our spiritual eyes fixed on Him of whom the ark speaks, the Lord Jesus Christ. As the author of Hebrews says, "Looking unto Jesus the author and finisher of our faith . . . for consider Him . . . lest you become weary and discouraged" (Heb. 12:2-3).

The TransJordan Tribes (vv. 12-13)

Joshua now mentions the army of the 2½ tribes who had acted according to their commitment to Moses in sending all their armed men over the Jordan to fight alongside those of the other 9½ tribes in the conquest of Canaan, "until the Lord has given rest to your brethren" (Deut. 3:20). We are told that 40,000 of their men equipped for war crossed Jordan "before the LORD to the plains of Jericho" for battle. They demonstrated their commitment to fight shoulder to shoulder with the other tribes in Canaan. Their wives and children stayed back with their flocks on the east side of Jordan.

However, not all of the TransJordan soldiers went. From the book of Numbers we learn that Reuben had 46,500 men, Gad 45,650, and Manasseh 32,200, of whom half (16,100) should have gone (Num. 1:21, 25, 35). Their combined armies should have numbered 108,250 soldiers. Although some probably stayed to guard their land, wives, and cattle, the numbers mentioned seem to indicate that there was not a full show of support when they crossed.

When the people of Israel saw that they were all safely over the Jordan, it says, "The LORD magnified Joshua in the sight of all Israel" as He had promised to do (v. 14, cf. 3:7). After they crossed the Jordan they finally and fully accepted Joshua as their leader. He had been faithful in the little details of every commandment from God. Now, in the light of that wonderful day, God gave him national recognition. He became like Moses to the people. The point is that Joshua was not seeking recognition, but rather seeking to please God in everything. Because he pleased the Lord, it was the Lord who gave him the recognition.

The Ark of the Testimony (vv. 15-17)

As with several other themes in this chapter we now find some additional facts about what has already been stated. We learned from verse 11 that the priests who carried the ark "crossed over" to the west bank. Now we see that the Lord specifically commanded Joshua to command the priests who were carrying the ark to "come up from Jordan" (vv. 15-17). Notice that for the first time in the book of Joshua the ark is referred to as "The ark of the Testimony" (v. 16). The word *testimony* is always used in the Old Testament to refer to God's covenant. The ark is called the ark of the Testimony because inside it was the Testimony, or Law, that God had inscribed on the two tables of stone and given to Moses (Ex. 25:21, 22). God's Law was to be the rule of life for them in Canaan.

The Return of the Floodwaters (v. 18)

When the "soles of the priests' feet touched the dry land," that is, the edge of where the floodwaters had been the day before, "the waters of the Jordan returned to their place and overflowed all its banks as before" (v. 18). The waters had receded as soon as the soles of the priests' feet had touched the edge of the river (3:15). Now the waters returned as soon as the soles of the priests' feet reached the western edge. God performed an enormous miracle that day! The way back into the wilderness was cut off. The whole nation was committed now to moving forward in conquest of the Promised Land.

The First Camp at Gilgal (vv. 19-20)

The date of the crossing is recorded as the tenth day of the first month. On this same day in the Hebrew calendar the lamb for the Passover had been selected (Ex. 12:3). In the next chapter we will see that they reinstituted the Passover on the fourteenth day when the Passover had been originally instituted (Ex. 12:6, 18).

The Israelites were now on the relatively flat land (called the plains of the Jordan) between the river and the steep hills behind Jericho. Somewhere in the five-mile stretch between the river and Jericho the Israelites set up their encampment at Gilgal. The exact location is not known, but it became an important base for the Israelites in their conquest of Canaan for many years to come. It may have been the same place as where Samuel judged and where Saul was anointed king (1 Sam. 7:16; 10:8; 11:14-15). If so, it endured as an important place for several centuries. Still later a place called Gilgal was condemned by the prophet Amos for its idolatry and the Israelites were forbidden to go there (Amos 4:4; 5:5).

"What are these stones?" (vv. 20-24)

Joshua closed that momentous day by setting up the twelve stones at Gilgal and making a speech to all the people. He knew the significance of the memorial pillar of stones for the coming generations and told the people what to say when their children saw the cairn or pillar and asked their fathers in the future saying, "What are these stones?" The fathers were to reply, "Israel crossed over this Jordan on dry land" (v. 22)—a summary statement that the fathers would likely expand it with more details.

Joshua connected the activity of the Lord when He "dried up" the waters of the Jordan to His previous activity when He "dried up" the Red Sea (v. 23). The whole movement of two million Israelites from Egypt to Canaan was bracketed by these two momentous miracles when God *dried up* both the Red

Sea and the Jordan. These two great miracles were not only to be a witness of God's power to the Israelites, but "that all the peoples of the earth may know the hand of the LORD, that it is mighty." The phrase "hand of the LORD" often refers to His powerful acts (Ex. 3:19; 6:1; Deut. 6:21; 7:8). Not only were the peoples of the world to know that God was mighty, the people of Israel were to respond by fearing God forever (v. 24).

In Conclusion

The crossing of the Jordan is a most instructive part of Israelite history as it teaches believers the spiritual step of moving into the place of God's blessing and victory. The important points of the lesson are the faith Israel needed to move out, the centrality of the ark as an illustration of Christ, and the need for their continued memory of what God had done in the years to come prompted by the two pillars of twelve stones.

Joshua 5

The Base Camp at Gilgal

When Jacob obeyed God in leaving Canaan to go down to Egypt, God had promised him that He would go with him and make his family into a great nation while they were there. Now they were back in the land, encamped at Gilgal. However, if they were to enjoy the blessings of the land they still had to face walled cities, strong armies, and giants. For the battles ahead they had to be prepared. Chapter 5 of Joshua recounts their preparations to take the land—preparations that were more spiritual in nature than military.

Gilgal became the base camp for their army and a temporary home for their families and livestock while the soldiers were taking one stronghold after another throughout the land. The first stronghold that they needed to take was Jericho, the city that controlled all the plains of the Jordan and was only a few miles away. But before they did that, God wanted them to face their spiritual condition. This chapter records two important rituals that they needed to observe—rituals that God had instituted on separate occasions many years earlier in their history. The first was circumcision, which was the sign of the covenant. The second was the Passover. The spiritual implications of both were essential to victory for God's people. When these were completed, God revealed Himself to Joshua, their commander, in a new way.

The Effect of the Crossing of the Jordan (v. 1)

One of God's purposes for the great miracle at the Jordan was that "all the peoples of the earth may know the hand of the LORD, that it is mighty" (4:24). The first verse of chapter 5 goes right on to tell how the kings of the Canaanites responded to that knowledge. The Amorites occupied the hill country, and the Canaanites lived both along the coast and in the Jordan valley (Num. 13:29). Rahab's report revealed that they already knew about how God helped them in crossing the Red Sea and defeating the Amorite kings, Sihon and Og. When they heard how God had dried up the Jordan and had brought the Israelites across the river, "their heart melted; and there was no spirit in them any longer" (v. 1). They became even more terrified of the Israelites though they had not yet met them in battle.

Two results came from this. First, it meant the invasion would be much easier than it might have been, because the Canaanites expected to be defeated. The second was that it allowed the males to be circumcised without fear of being attacked. During those three days the Israelite males would have been incapacitated and vulnerable, in no condition to fight. God's sovereign control over the whole situation is evident.

From the human perspective it was the worst possible time to do such a thing. Military strategy demanded that after the crossing of the Jordan and finding the enemies terrorized, the Israelite army should have struck a paralyzing blow at the enemy right away. But God knew that their spiritual preparations were more important than military strategy. They were not yet ready to glorify God in the battles; they needed to be completely consecrated first. The same principle applies to God's people today. Many of us are tempted to think that what matters most is to following the sure steps to success laid out by an expert at a seminar. But in reality the most important thing in living a victorious life is abiding in Christ.

The Renewal of the Rite of Circumcision (vv. 2-8)

The first of the necessary preliminaries for the conquest was the renewal of the rite of circumcision. In crossing the Jordan they had paid special attention to the *ark* of the covenant. Now they were called to pay attention to the *mark* of the covenant, circumcision. The verse begins, "At that time" (v. 2). They had just taken a huge step of faith in crossing the Jordan. They were on the verge of engaging the enemy. The timing was important. Having crossed over Jordan to the *land* of the covenant, they needed to obey the *terms* of the covenant in order to inherit the *blessings* of the covenant.

The Background of Circumcision

When Abraham arrived in Canaan God told him to look in all directions "for all the land which you see I give to you and your descendants forever" (Gen. 13:15). He promised that Abraham would have many descendants and that they would inherit the land of the Canaanites. The two major elements in the covenant were the "seed" (descendants) and the "land." Later, when Abraham's faith was stronger, God confirmed his covenant promises with a special ceremony and an oath (Gen. 15:1-21). Even later, God told Abraham that he and his descendants should observe the covenant by instituting the rite of circumcision. Circumcision was a *sign* of the covenant between Himself and Abraham (Gen. 17:11). First there had been the *explanation* of the covenant, then the *confirmation* of the covenant, and finally the *sign* of the covenant. Abraham obeyed by circumcising all the male men in his household (Gen. 17:26-27).

The Significance of Circumcision

Since the time when the Israelites had crossed the Red Sea, no male who was born in the wilderness—a whole generation under forty years of age—had been circumcised. Therefore, when they had reached the land of the covenant, it was absolutely necessary they observe the sign of the covenant. Being circumcised was the outward demonstration of their faith in God and compliance with the covenant He had made with them. Down through history, circumcision has marked Israel's descendants as God's special people and reminded them that they are the beneficiaries of the covenant He made with Abraham.

Moses had reminded the Israelites in the wilderness that there were spiritual overtones to circumcision. He said, "What does the LORD your God require of you, but to fear the LORD your God, to walk in His ways and to love Him, to serve the LORD your God with all your heart and with all your soul. . . . The LORD delighted only in your fathers, to love them; and He chose their descendants after them, you above all peoples. Therefore circumcise the foreskin of your heart, and be stiff-necked no longer" (Deut. 10:12, 15-16).

Thus circumcision signified two things to the Israelites. First, that as the descendants of Abraham, they were set apart as a people with whom God had made a covenant. As a people they were the object of His love and the means of His purpose of blessing the world. But circumcision was also a sign that symbolized a separation from the sins of the flesh, signifying that they were to live their lives according to the holy standards of the Law of God which had been clearly given to them in the wilderness.

The Command to Circumcise (vv. 2-5)

The Lord said to Joshua: "Make flint knives for yourself" (v. 2). It is interesting that they used flint knives, for they lived in the Bronze Age, when bronze was used freely for implements and cutting tools. God, however, had told them to use flint, which may actually have made a better and sharper surgical tool. Flint is mentioned in Scripture in only one other place—in connection with the circumcision of Moses' son (cf. Ex. 4:25). The flint knives used in Joshua's time may have been special knives for this ceremonial purpose. The name of the place was called Gibeath-Haaraloth, which is translated in the text as "hill of the foreskins." It was the first of two names for the site. The other was Gilgal (v. 3, cf. v. 9).

The Reason for Circumcision (v. 6)

God said "Circumcise the sons of Israel *again the second time.*" Joshua obeyed God's command, and all those born in the wilderness were circumcised. When the Israelites were circumcised they were affirming the solemn contract that God had made with them. They were setting themselves apart to love God and to serve Him. It symbolized their separation from the sins of the flesh and their consecration to God to live a holy life. All the people who came out of Egypt had been circumcised (v. 5). But they had all been "consumed" or destroyed in the wilderness because "they did not obey the voice of the LORD" (v. 6). Physical circumcision alone was not enough. If they were going to enjoy the Promised Land full of "milk and honey" (v. 6), they needed to be circumcised in heart as well as body. It was a solemn warning to Joshua's men that they too might fail to inherit the land if they failed to live out the consecrated obedience that their circumcision signified. Therefore, Joshua circumcised all the males in Israel who had not been circumcised (v. 7).

The Reproach is Rolled Away (v. 9)

When Joshua had completed the circumcision the Lord spoke again to him: "This day I have rolled away the reproach of Egypt from you. Therefore the name of the place is called Gilgal to this day" (v. 9). The name "Gilgal" comes from a verb that means "to roll." What some, however, are puzzled by is the meaning of the phrase "the reproach of Egypt." This phrase is best seen as the sarcastic taunting of Egyptians when the Israelites were leaving Egypt that God could not care for them and that they would all die in the wilderness. Moses had feared this. He expressed his concern to God in Exodus 32:12, "Why should the Egyptians speak and say, 'He brought them out to harm them, to kill them in the mountains?'" He also prayed on another occasion, "Do not look on the stubbornness of this people . . . lest the land from which you brought us should say, 'Because the LORD was not able to bring them to the land which He promised them, and because He hated them'" (Deut. 9:27-28).

Now that the children of Israel were actually in the Promised Land and had just rededicated themselves to God by being circumcised, what the Egyptians had thought was impossible, God had accomplished. The reproach, or mockery, of the Egyptians could never be hurled at them again. The Lord Himself had rolled it away. They were free from slavery, and they were in the land of the covenant.

The Spiritual Lesson of Circumcision

Gilgal's great lesson for the believer is that if we want to enjoy the victory and the blessing of our inheritance in Christ, we need to put off the sins of the flesh. The Israelites had crossed the Jordan keeping the ark central both in the riverbed, the place of death, and in crossing over to Canaan, the place of resurrection. Thus, the believer recognizes his death with Christ and his resurrection with Him to newness of life (Rom. 6:1-4). Just as the Israelites were circumcised, symbolizing the putting off of the flesh, so believers who have been buried and raised with Christ are to "reckon" themselves to be dead to sin and alive to God. They are not to let sin reign in their bodies or obey its lusts (Rom. 6:11-12). This truth is further explained in Colossians: "In Him you were also circumcised with the circumcision made without hands, by putting off the body of the sins of the flesh" (Col. 2:11). That is what we are to do. Paul elaborates, "Therefore put to death your members which are on the earth: fornication, uncleanness, passion, evil desire, and covetousness, which is idolatry" (Col. 3:5). He also exhorts believers to "put off all these: anger, wrath, malice, blasphemy, filthy language . . ." (Col. 3:8).

The Celebration of the Passover (v. 10)

The next thing that happened at Gilgal was that the Israelites kept the Passover. This is only the third time they are recorded as having kept it. The first occasion was the initial one in Egypt, when God had instituted the feast (Exodus 12). They also kept it when they reached Mount Sinai in the first year of their wilderness journey (Num. 9:1-5). No other occasion is mentioned until this one, here in Canaan. Keeping the Passover after renewing the rite of circumcision was appropriate, for God had ordained that "no uncircumcised person shall eat it" (Ex. 12:48). They kept the Passover on the fourteenth day of the month (v. 10), four days after they crossed the river.

The central point in the Passover was their deliverance from Egypt. Subsequent Passover feasts looked back to this deliverance and forward to the coming of the Redeemer. When the Lamb of God was sacrificed at Golgotha, celebrating the Passover feast as such was no longer a commandment that had to be kept. For the Israelites, the Passover was a time of worship and celebration, much as the Lord's Supper is for Christian believers today in local churches. It must have led to a wonderful and happy celebration four days after they had entered the Promised Land. Even with Jericho so nearby, they could enter into the sentiment of what the psalmist David would write many years later: "You prepare a table before me in the presence of my enemies" (Ps. 23:5). It was, no doubt, the happiest day in the life of the nation to this point. More than fourteen hundred years later the greater Joshua was with His disciples at the Passover, and they became a new people of God under the new covenant (Matt. 26:26-28).

Eating the Produce of the Land (v. 11)

The day after the Passover, Israel began to enjoy the fruit of the land. The grain fields and the vineyards of the Canaanites were now ripe because it was springtime—harvest time in Canaan. The Israelites were therefore free to gather all they needed. God had timed their arrival perfectly. They had not been able to roast kernels of grain or bake unleavened bread from wheat flour for forty years. Now God was giving it to them to enjoy, and undoubtedly it gave sheer pleasure after all those years of manna.

For us, the significance of their feasting on the grain of the land is that believers entering into their inheritance are to feed on Christ the Living Bread, risen and glorified (John 6:53-58). He is the kernal of wheat which fell into the ground and died but which has brought forth fruit. When we discover that Christ is our life and begin to feed on Him as the riches of His grace are revealed, we begin to enjoy the life that God has planned for us. Just as the measure of the food available to the Israelites was the abundance of the land itself, so the measure of what is available in Christ is as great as the infinite God Himself. They ate that which they had neither plowed nor planted. Parched grain and unleavened bread were actually just the foretaste of what was to come. In the days ahead they would be able to enjoy "houses full of all good things which [they] did not fill, hewn out wells which [they] did not dig, vineyards and olive trees which [they] did not plant" (Deut. 6:11). John could say of the riches of Christ for the believer, "Of His fullness have we all received, and grace for grace" (John 1:16).

The Cessation of the Manna (vv. 11-12)

For forty years the staple of their diet had been the manna God had sent down every morning, six days a week. Now that the ark of the covenant was in the land, the mark of the covenant had been renewed, the celebration of the covenant had been observed, and the food of the covenant land had been eaten, "The manna ceased on the day after they had eaten the produce of the land." Their wilderness living was over, and their Canaan living had begun. The ceasing of the manna was an important transition, illustrated by its repetition in these verses. Three times in these two verses we are told that they ate the produce of the land, and twice in verse 12 we read that the manna had ceased.

The miraculous would give way to the ordinary. The spectacular was their kindergarten experience. God wanted them to mature. They would fulfill the creation mandate to till the ground and obtain their food by working for it in the ordinary way. It was to be the ordinary food, at first taken from the Canaanites, but in subsequent years planted and harvested by the Israelites. The principle is also true in regard to the Lord's work. Too many workers think that God ought to supply all their wants by miraculous means. They shy away from working for their living by the sweat of their brow. The work ethic was true for Israel and is still true for Christian workers. The fruit of Canaan can be enjoyed if we are willing to follow God's ordained ways.

The new era of Canaan living began at a specific point in time. Note that "the day" is specified twice and "that year" is stated once. What year? It signaled the end of the forty years in the wilderness and was probably 1406 BC. At the beginning of the Hebrew month of Nissan God spoke to Joshua. On the fifth of that month they moved their camp to the east bank of Jordan. On the tenth of Nissan they crossed the river and set up the two memorials. On the eleventh they renewed the rite of circumcision. On the fourteenth they celebrated the Passover. On the fifteenth they ate the produce of the land. The next day the manna stopped. The forty years of eating manna was over, and their new life had begun (Ex. 16:35; cf. Josh. 5:6, 12).

The Commander of the Lord's Army (vv. 13-15)

Jericho stood in the way of access to the land of Canaan. There was no way around it to get to the valleys behind that led up into the hill country. The nation comprised of two million people who of necessity had to move very slowly. Joshua had evidently gone out to reconnoiter "by Jericho," no doubt to take note of its defenses. Not since his spy mission thirty-eight years before had he seen the awesome sight of a fortified city with its huge gates shut. As Israel's leader, Joshua had tremendous responsibility on his shoulders. The Israelites had no means of attacking those walls. He had no idea how to defeat a walled city, militarily speaking. Humanly speaking, they didn't appear to have a chance.

This final episode in chapter 5, like the others, has to do with the spiritual preparation for the conquest. Circumcision and the Passover had to do with the people's holiness and commitment to God. This episode follows the theme of personal holiness, but it had to do with Joshua's own relationship with God. As the commander of Israel's army, he met the Commander of the Lord's army. Then follows a scene very much like that of Moses at the burning bush where Moses met the same divine Being. Joshua "lifted up his eyes" and saw a "Man ... with His sword drawn" in front of him (v. 13). Joshua did not know who the "Man" was at first, so he approached Him.

Meeting the Commander (v. 13)

Joshua challenged the Man with a question similar to "Halt, who goes there, friend or foe?" He asked, "Are You for us or for our adversaries?" (v. 13). Joshua was no doubt ready for a duel, to meet steel with steel. The Man with the drawn sword answered, "No, but as Commander of the army of the LORD." What Joshua saw was a *theophany*, an appearance of God. He was talking with none other than the second Person of the Trinity.

The Man did not directly answer Joshua's question, but He said something much more important. He said in effect, "No, I am not the enemy's soldier, nor am I a friendly soldier. I command the armies of heaven." The sword in His hand evidenced the Lord's part in the coming battles with the Canaanites, it symbolized the judgment with which He was about to avenge the corrupt pagan people whose wickedness had been multiplying for hundreds of years and was now "ripe" for judgment (Gen. 15:16). In the invasion of Canaan, God was actually accomplishing two things: judging the Canaanites for their wickedness while giving His people a homeland in perpetuity.

This was one of the pre-incarnation appearances of the Lord Jesus Christ. These appearances were quite varied in their nature. To Abraham He came as a passer by and partook of a meal to share some information (Gen. 18:1-8). To Jacob He came as a wrestler, to bring the schemer to a place of weakness and dependence (Gen. 32:24-32). To Shadrach, Meshach, and Abednego He came as a friend in the fiery furnace (Dan. 3:25). To Joshua He came as the Commander of the hosts of heaven to assure him of victory.

Yahweh's heavenly army consists of the host of angels under His command. It fits the situation better here to see His army as made up of heavenly beings who would be on Israel's side during the conquest. The Lord wanted Joshua to understand that, beyond his own human army, he had the hosts of heaven on his side. God often is referred to as the "Lord of Hosts;" thus, all the angelic hosts were there under Yahweh's command.

Joshua Worships (v. 14)

When Joshua saw Him and heard Him speak, he suddenly realized to whom he was speaking, so he fell on his face and said "What does my Lord say to His servant?" Though Joshua was in command of a nation and a large army, he knew that he was only a servant. Before he could properly lead God's people to victory he needed to understand his true relationship to God his Master ("Lord" here is *Adonai,* which means "Master"). As God's servant his task was to lead God's people under God's authority. This principle (human leaders understanding their place as God's servants) is vital for Christian leaders to accept. Before they try to lead, they must see themselves in the light of God's majesty and infinite holiness. And, like Joshua, these leaders must approach Him with the attitude of submission, willing to take orders themselves.

Joshua realized that no matter the size of the enemy army, God's army was infinitely bigger and more powerful. Jehovah would give him victory over the enemies and accomplish the impossible. Moses had learned this at the burning bush (Ex. 3:1-8). Isaiah learned it when he had the vision of God (Isaiah 6). Paul learned it through his vision on the road to Damascus (Acts 9).

"The place where you stand is holy" (v. 15)

While Joshua was on his face in worship, the Commander said to him, "Take your sandal off your foot, for the place where you stand is holy." The Lord had given this same command to Moses (Ex. 3:5). What made the place holy was that the Lord was there, and Joshua had to recognize that it was a place "set apart." Through his position of worship and his removing of his sandals Joshua acknowledged God's sovereign leadership. He was putting himself on God's side and under God's control.

In Conclusion

The great lesson to be learned from Joshua 5 is that the people of God needed to be prepared spiritually before they could have victory over their enemies. Review the many preparatory events at Gilgal recorded in this chapter, all of which are instructive for the people of God today. First, the renewal of the rite of circumcision illustrates their commitment to God and His promises, as well as the putting off of the flesh. Second, the keeping of the Passover exemplifies how their deliverance from the power of Egypt was effected through the power of the blood of the lamb. Third, eating the food native to Canaan and the cessation of the manna illustrated the forward steps believers must take to enjoy the fruits of victory, leaving behind their dependence on the miraculous. Finally, Joshua's encounter with the divine Person illustrates the sovereign control of a holy God and the place we have at His feet as humble servants.

Joshua 6

The Destruction of Jericho

The first five chapters of Joshua cover Israel's preparation for the conquest of Canaan. God had "prepared" the Canaanite people, too, by giving them a fear of the Israelites. He had also readied Joshua by encouraging him to hold fast to the Law, to implicitly obey the commands of God, and to understand that the Lord had a huge unseen army that would give him the victory. Finally, He had prepared the people by miraculously bringing them across the Jordan, focusing their attention on the ark of the covenant, and sanctifying them through the renewal of the rite of circumcision.

Three Strategic Battles

Israel was now entering its first phase for the conquest of Canaan. This phase began with the destruction of Jericho and reached its climax with the renewal of the covenant in Mount Ebal (Joshua 6-8). Three battles are recorded in this section. Israel won the first at Jericho, lost the second at Ai, and came back to defeat Ai. However, if we are to understand the Spirit of God's intent in guiding the author, it is necessary to keep in mind that the spiritual side of the conquest is once again more important than the actual battles. Israel won or lost each battle on the basis of their relationship with God at the time, not their military expertise.

Jericho: Guardian of Access to the Heartland

Jericho was an Amorite (also referred to as Canaanite) fortress city guarding the main access to the land of Canaan from the Jordan Valley. It was located on the western edge of the plains of the Jordan, which abruptly give way to steep hills and valleys to the west. Access to the center of the country was gained by the "Way of the Wilderness," a valley that led up to the high country in the center of the land where Ai and Bethel were located (8:15). Another valley led from near Jericho up to a point just south of Jerusalem where the modern road is situated today. These valleys were only about fifteen miles long, but because of the rugged terrain they formed the only good access to the central hills. Overthrowing Jericho, therefore, was key to invading Canaan.

Jericho was the fortress of a city-state, one of many in Canaan. It had its own king and ruled over the surrounding area where the people practiced farming, viticulture, and the raising of livestock. When danger threatened, all the people from the citi-state would retreat to the fortress for protection and to wait for an opportunity to attack the enemy. The fear of the Israelites would probably have already driven all the area's inhabitants inside the walls. Modern archeologists have closely examined the site of ancient Jericho. They have determined that the city covered eight acres and was surrounded by two very high parallel walls about fifteen feet apart. If the enemy breached the first wall, the citizens had a second line of defense. It was the sight of walls like those of Jericho that caused the spies sent by Moses many years earlier to say, "The cities are great and fortified up to heaven" (Deut. 1:28).

The conquest of Jericho is not only an actual historical event but a highly significant one to the people of God today as a dramatic illustration of faith. We learn from Hebrews that, "By faith the walls of Jericho fell down after they were encircled for seven days" (Heb. 11:30). Those walls were not brought down by battering rams and siege engines, but by faith in the power of the Almighty God. God's people are often faced with the spiritual strongholds of the enemy. Christians have weapons for spiritual warfare which are "mighty in God for pulling down strongholds" (2 Cor. 10:4). When we are skilled in the use of the sword of the Spirit and have learned to obey our Commander implicitly, then arguments and every high thing that exalts itself against the knowledge of God can be brought into captivity (2 Cor. 4:5). Jericho pictures a stronghold of Satan. All his "fortresses" that hinder us from increasing our knowledge of God need to be destroyed, just as Jericho needed to be destroyed before the Israelites could proceed into the land.

Breeching the Walls

The ancients used different methods, either singly or in combination, to breach walls of a fortified city. Battering rams were used to smash a hole through the walls after repeated ramming—often for weeks on end. If possible, tunnels would be dug under the wall. Sometimes a siege was set up around the city to starve the people into surrender. The Israelites had no experience whatsoever in facing walled cities. But God had plans to destroy it that included none of the above methods.

"Jericho was securely shut up" (v. 1)

The account begins by describing the city as "securely shut up." The RSV translates it as "shut up from within and without," which is parallel to the second statement, "None went out, and none came in." The residents of Jericho made sure that no enemy could slip in undetected, or defectors leave. The fact that the city was, in man's view, impregnable underlies the greatness of the miracle that God was about to perform. The contrast was similar to the miracle of chapter 3 where the divine author draws our attention to the fact that the Jordan had swelled to capacity just before God performed the miracle of drying it up. The statement about the city's security prepares us to marvel at God's wonderful act of power.

Instructions for Capturing Jericho (vv. 2-5)

God first promised Joshua that He would give the king of Jericho and all the "mighty men of valor" into his hand (v. 2). It may be that these words are a continuation of the conversation that the "Commander of the Lord's army" had with Joshua in chapter 5:13-15, but chapter 6 is usually considered a separate episode. The Lord did not say anything to Joshua about using military weapons. Instead, He gave instructions about a ceremonial ritual in which the Israelite soldiers would simply march around the city.

The priests were to carry the ark at the center of the procession. For six consecutive days, seven priests were to march ahead of the ark bearing and blowing seven trumpets made of ram's horns. They were to be accompanied by the army. From Numbers 26 we learn that the Israelites had 600,000 armed men. We do not know how many took part in this attack (there would not have been room for 600,000), but more than likely they fielded enough men to completely encircle the city during each day's circuit. On the seventh day the armies and the priests were to march around the city seven times instead of just once. When they had completed the seventh circuit of the city that day, the trumpeters were to make a long blast with the ram's horn trumpets. As soon as the army heard the long blast they were all to "shout with a great shout" (v. 5). God then promised Joshua that at that moment, the fortress walls of the city would "fall down flat. And the people shall go up every man straight before him." These verses remind us that Yahweh did three things crucial to the victory: He instilled *the fear of the Lord* in the minds of the enemy (v. 1). He gave the Israelites *the promise of the Lord* (v. 2). Finally, He outlined *the strategy of the Lord* for Joshua to win the victory (vv. 3-5).

The Significance of the Number Seven

The number seven is used so many times in this chapter that the reader must wonder about its significance. There were seven priests, seven trumpets, seven days, and seven circuits around the city on the seventh day. The word "seven" is used fourteen times in this chapter. In Scripture, the number seven signifies divine completion and perfection. Scripture begins with the account of the seven days of creation and ends with the seven last things (described in Revelation 19-20), with dozens of "sevens" throughout. In this chapter the number seven symbolizes the complete victory that Yahweh would give His people and the complete destruction of Jericho that pictures God's just judgment of sin. Even before He had told Joshua how to win, God had said that He had already given Jericho, its king, and its mighty men of valor, into Joshua's hand (v. 2). The victory was won before they started. Christians, too, are "more than conquerors through Him who loved us" (Rom. 8:37).

Joshua Speaks to the Priests (v. 6)

Joshua immediately acted on God's clear instructions. He called the priests to take up the ark and for seven of them to take their positions in front of it with their trumpets (v. 6). Notice that he called the priests first and made sure that the ark was in the right place. The ram's horn trumpet (called a *shofar*) makes a mournful sound that carries well. They are still used by Jews for certain ceremonies today. These trumpets were used at Mount Sinai to announce God's presence to the people when He was about to reveal the Ten Commandments. When they heard the shofar trumpets, they knew that God was there, and they trembled (Ex. 19:16, 19). Interestingly they did not use the silver trumpets that were specifically used to call them to war (Num. 10:9). The Israelites, however, were not declaring war at this time, but were celebrating the presence of God.

The "men of war" were to march around the city. These were the soldiers of Israel, not the women, youth, and children, who were to remain in Gilgal at the camp (v. 3). As they marched, the trumpets blew. All the people in Jericho would hear them. Each day for six days the priests in front of the ark blew those trumpets for as long as it took to go around the walls of the city. Just as the ark had been the central feature of the crossing of Jordan, so it was the central feature of the conquest of Jericho. It is mentioned ten times in this chapter. The Israelites marching around the city were to understand that they would be victorious because God was with them. The Amorites in Jericho were to understand that their fortress city and all their armor was no match for Yahweh, the God of Israel, represented by the ark.

God told Joshua that on the seventh day they were to march around the city seven times with the priests blowing the trumpets. The priests were then to make a long continuous blast on the trumpets. When the army heard the blast, they were to "shout with a great shout." God promised that He would then bring those walls down. Only then were the soldiers to move in to destroy the city.

Joshua Charges the People (v. 7)

After speaking to the priests (v. 6), Joshua spoke to the people, that is, the army (v. 7). He told them to proceed to "advance" with armed men placed ahead of the ark as they marched around the city. The ark is still very much in focus. In verse 6 it is referred to as the ark of the covenant, stressing its promise for the people's future good. In verse 7 it is called the ark of the Lord, stressing Yahweh's presence among them.

The author moves very slowly with the narrative to heighten the effect, just as he did in chapters 3 and 4 describing the crossing of Jordan. First, God spoke to Joshua about what to do (vv. 1-5). Then Joshua told the priests and the people what to do, adding that there was to be an armed escort going before the ark (vv. 6-7). Mention is now made of another escort of armed men following behind the ark (vv. 8-9). In each step there is a little bit more information is added to make the climax more dramatic.

The Instruction to be Silent (vv. 8-10)

The whole scene is described for the third time, but one more command is added. The huge company of soldiers both in front of and behind the ark was to march in silence. The only noise heard was to be coming from the trumpets continually being blown to draw everyone's attention to the ark. They were to maintain that silence for six days, "until the day" that Joshua would tell the priests to give the one blast, when he would give the command to shout.

Notice that emphasis is put on their keeping silent in three ways: Joshua said, "You shall not shout or make any noise with your voice, nor shall any word proceed out of your mouth" (v. 10). Shouting in the Old Testament indicated two things, both of which were appropriate in this situation. It could be a cry of alarm or a war cry (e.g. Judg. 7:21), and it could be a glad cry of praise to God (e.g. Ps. 95:1-2; 100:1). When the time came to shout, it would both frighten the inhabitants of Jericho and be a means of expressing praise to God for the victory.

The Six Days of Encirclement (vv. 11-17)

After three preliminary accounts describing the plan of encircling the city, the actual event is finally recorded. Watching from the walls, the people of Jericho must have been mystified as they observed the scene. With no sound except for trumpets, they were no doubt filled with apprehension as to the significance of the ark. They probably thought it contained an image of their God. They could not have known that it contained the holy moral standards God demanded and that God's stern judgment was about to fall on them because of their wickedness.

Whatever the people of Jericho were thinking, the Israelites had their own thoughts. Maybe they were becoming impatient. After all, if God were going to cause the walls of Jericho to collapse, why not do it the first day? But day after day they did the same thing—march from camp, march around the city, and return to camp. God was testing their patience along with their faith. The author of Hebrews tells us it is through faith and patience that the victorious ones inherited the promises of God (Heb. 6:12). God is typically not in a hurry by man's standards, but His timing is always perfect. Sometimes God has to remind us, "Be still, and know that I am God" (Ps. 46:10). Just as Naaman had to wait until he had completed seven immersions in the Jordan before he was healed of his leprosy, so the Israelites had to wait until the seventh day of circling around Jericho before seeing the walls come down. After the seventh circuit on the seventh day, a long blast on the trumpets was made and Joshua proclaimed, "Shout, for the LORD has given you the city!" (v. 16).

Things Doomed to Destruction (v. 18)

Joshua leaves his readers in suspense after giving the command to shout. The consequence of that shout is not described until verse 20. In between, he speaks of the warning he gave his army about taking the accursed things in Jericho. Exactly when Joshua warned them is not stated, but it could hardly have been in the sequence cited in chapter 6. That would place it right at the moment when the shout went up with the troops surrounding the whole city. Explicit instructions would hardly have been possible at that point. The warning was probably given at the same time as the other instructions.

The city of Jericho was doomed. Joshua literally told them that the city was "doomed by the LORD." The word "doomed," sometimes translated "devoted," means "to be irrevocably consecrated, to be under the ban so that it could not be redeemed or returned." Jericho had been "doomed" by the Lord to destruction and was therefore was to be completely destroyed (cf. Deut. 13:16). It is an illustration of the truth that all sin is condemned by our holy God, and He is entitled to judge it. Nothing in Jericho was to be salvaged, neither man, woman, child, animal, nor goods.

Two Exceptions to the Judgment on Jericho (vv. 17-19)

There was to be one exception to the judgment on the people of Jericho and another regarding the goods in Jericho. The first exception concerned Rahab and her family (v. 17), because of their faith. Rahab had confessed her faith by words and actions. Her family demonstrated a solid faith by waiting inside the house for more than a week, believing they would be spared the destruction that was coming on every other house and person in Jericho.

The other exception dealt with precious metals the soldiers might find in Jericho. Joshua informed them that God had consecrated these to Himself and that whatever gold, silver, bronze, or iron things they found were to be taken and stored in the "treasury of the LORD" (v. 19). It is not known where this treasury was located. The possessions of the Canaanites were cursed, just as the people themselves were cursed. Earlier, Moses had carefully instructed the Israelite army that they were to completely destroy the Canaanites. If they did not destroy them, the idol worshipping Canaanites would then teach the Israelites "to do according to all the abominations which they have done for their gods" (see Deut. 20:16-18).

For this solemn reason Joshua now reiterated the warnings that Moses had given them: "Keep yourselves from the accursed things, lest you become accursed" (v. 18). The soldiers might be tempted to take some of the spoils for themselves when they entered the city. God told them through Joshua that they were not to take anything for themselves in Jericho—no clothing, no jewelry, no valuables—nothing. Take note that four times in verse 18 the word "accursed" is used. If they touched anything accursed in Jericho, they would become accursed and bring "trouble" on the camp of Israel. In later battles they were allowed to acquire the spoils, but not in Jericho (Deut. 20:14). God, it seems, looked at Jericho as a kind of "firstfruits" of the land, reckoning it devoted to Him as an offering. It is for this reason that Achan's sin of acquiring some goods for himself (recorded in chapter 7) was so serious.

The Destruction of Jericho (vv. 20-21)

The story now reaches its climax. The middle of verse 20 records, "And it happened." What "happened" is described with a few abrupt details. The *priests blew* the long blast on the trumpets. *Joshua commanded* the people to shout. The *people shouted* with a great shout and suddenly the wall all around the city "fell down flat." We do not know whether God caused an earthquake to occur at this precise moment or how He accomplished the miracle. With the walls down, the soldiers surrounding the city were free to enter it. As they clambered over the rubble of the walls they "utterly destroyed all that was in the city, both man and woman, young and old," even all the animals (v. 21).

The complete collapse of the walls at the exact moment when the people shouted was the essence of the miracle. One single verse is all that Joshua uses to describe it (v. 21). We should keep in mind that it was not the collapse of the wall that is emphasized in this chapter but the spiritual preparations that preceded it. When the Israelites were spiritually prepared, God brought down those walls. It was "by faith" that the walls of Jericho fell down, "after they were encircled for seven days" (Heb. 11:30).

Rahab is Rescued (vv. 22-25)

The walls of Jericho had collapsed everywhere except Rahab's house. That in itself was a miracle. Joshua told the two spies who had earlier made the oath with Rahab (2:14) that they were responsible to find her house and bring her and her relatives out. They would not have needed to look for the red cord because the only part of the wall still standing was her house!

The men rescued them and "left them outside the camp of Israel." Like everyone else in Jericho, they were Gentiles. Though they had become believers in Israel's God, they were not yet incorporated into the people of Israel. They were still looked upon as "unclean" and would need to be ceremonially cleansed (Num. 5:1-4). They would be required to declare their faith in Yahweh, submit to the Law, and have the men circumcised. Their temporary place outside the camp was not to last long. God graciously gave Rahab a husband named Salmon. She became the mother of Boaz, one of the main characters in the book of Ruth, and she gained a place in the ancestry of the Lord Jesus. Rahab was still alive when the book of Joshua was written (v. 25).

The Curse on Jericho (vv. 26-27)

Joshua warned the people by pronouncing a curse on anyone who would rebuild Jericho. Many years after this pronouncement a man from Bethel named Hiel did rebuild Jericho. He felt the curse of God when two of his sons died in building its foundations and gates, "according to the word of the LORD which he had spoken through Joshua the son of Nun" (1 Kings 16:34). God's presence with Joshua and God's work through him caused his fame to spread. "So the LORD was with Joshua, and his fame spread throughout all the country" (v. 27). Joshua's greatest reward was that the Lord was with him.

In Conclusion

The lessons of Joshua 6 are important for us. Like Joshua and the Israelites, we live in a world under judgment. If we are to live lives of victory we must follow the Lord Jesus Christ, just as the Israelite army followed the ark. They had to be patient waiting for the Lord's timing, and like them we often must accompany our faith with patience. When the moment of victory came it was the Lord who accomplished it. Israel simply moved in on the victory that He had already won. It is the same for us: we live in the wake of the victory over sin and death that Christ won at Calvary.

JOSHUA 7

Defeat at Ai

The first phase of the Israelites' conquest of Canaan was accomplished perfectly—or so it seemed. What seemed like an untarnished victory in chapter 6 is turned upside down in chapter 7. The chapter begins with a summary statement for the reader explaining that the events at Jericho were marred by a serious problem in God's sight. The Israelites did not learn the extent of the problem until God allowed them to be defeated and humiliated.

Sin in the Camp (v. 1)

The first verse begins, "But the children of Israel committed a trespass regarding the accursed things," the things, that is, that were devoted to destruction by God. The guilty person is named and his lineage traced back four generations. His name was Achan the son of Carmi, the son of Zabdi, the son of Zerah from the tribe of Judah, which was the leading tribe of Israel. His sin was so serious that it would affect the whole family—indeed, the whole nation.

Achan had obviously been a member of the task force given the special duty of collecting the gold and silver when Jericho was sacked and burned. Under cover of smoke and in the confusion of the battle, he had evidently not been able to resist taking a quantity of gold and of silver, as well as a fine Babylonian garment. Maybe he desired prestige and recognition. Maybe he rationalized his theft, saying to himself, "Who will miss a couple of bars of gold and silver, and why burn the coat? Taking it is not going to harm anyone else, is it? If it is burned, it is no good to anyone."

Satan was no doubt active in Achan's temptation. And although Achan did not seem to have calculated the seriousness of it, God did. God's anger burned against the sons of Israel. Their sin would be justly recompensed. The reader is fully informed before the history unfolds.

God's Anger Burns

While Achan clearly seems to have acted alone in his sin, the divine Author inspired Joshua to attribute the act to all the people. All were included in the first statement that the "children of Israel" had acted unfaithfully. All were under God's discipline (v. 1). One man's sin affected them all. The Lord later told Joshua that the guilty man had "transgressed [overstepped] the covenant of the LORD" (v. 15). Any act by one person that violated the covenant relationship of God with His people meant that the nation was no longer in compliance. Achan's sin had defiled the holiness of all Israel, and they all would suffer as a result. This same principle applies to the local church where the unjudged sin of an individual affects and infects the whole church. Paul wrote, "Do you not know that a little leaven leavens the whole lump?" (1 Cor. 5:6). The Israelites would pay a corporate price, but Achan was also individually responsible and would pay a higher price. The word translated "burn" in verse 1 (as well the words "blaze" and "kindle") is used several times in the Bible to refer to the Lord's anger against the sins of His people (cf. Num. 11:1, 10). As His anger had burned against them in the wilderness, so it burned against them after Achan's sin at Jericho.

The phrase "committed a trespass" (v. 1) carries the concept of betraying a trust. We use the term "unfaithful" today when a marriage partner violates his or her vows to be true to the other with respect to sexual intimacy. Such unfaithfulness results in a broken relationship. So here, the relationship between the Israelites and God was broken by their unfaithfulness to the covenant. It could only be restored by discovering the cause, removing it completely, and renewing the covenant. Thus, this chapter and the next deal with the discovery of the sin, the removal of the offending person, and the renewal of the covenant. The application to the sins of believers as to the need to confess sin, to yield to divine discipline, and to move on in our relationship with God, will be very evident.

Joshua Sends Spies to Ai (vv. 2-3)

Ai was a small fortress city at the top of a wadi, or valley, leading from Jericho to the hill country near Bethel. Just as Jericho guarded the lower end of the valley leading to the central hill country in Canaan, so Ai guarded the upper end of the same valley and the way to the central part of Canaan. A major road runs up that same valley today. Ai, as a fortress city, was small but important to the Israelites as a key to their penetrating the land and claiming their inheritance. Joshua's battle plan was to divide the land in half (between north and south) to prevent a united Canaanite defense against them. The site of Ai is specified in this chapter as "near Bethhaven and east of Bethel," but the exact site today has yet to be positively identified by archeologists. Some think it might be at Beitin in the general area of Bethel.

The Report of the Spies (v. 3)

Once again, as he had done before the battle of Jericho, Joshua sent men from Jericho to spy out the land. When they returned they gave a report stating that the conquest of that city would be a simple matter. They concluded, "Let about two or three thousand men go up . . . and attack Ai . . . for the people of

Ai are few." Their report to Joshua should be compared with the report of the Jericho spies, for there is a marked difference. The Jericho spies concluded from Rahab's testimony that Yahweh had given them the land because He had caused the Canaanites to be terrified (2:9). They came back to Joshua reporting that "truly the LORD has delivered all the land into our hands" (2:24). Their report placed God in the center of their thinking, but the report of the Ai spies did not even mention God. They presumed that, humanly speaking, two or three thousand soldiers would be sufficient to easily take the city, "for the people of Ai are few." The valley ascended more than three thousand feet in the fifteen miles from Jericho to Bethel, so they said, "Do not weary all the people [to go] there."

While it is not stated whether their recommendation was based on faith or pride, it is evident that pride was the prime factor. Sometimes pride masquerades as faith. Sometimes pride blinds us, because it makes the enemy appear smaller than he is. (Unlike pride, fear makes the enemy appear bigger than he really is.) The Israelites presumed that God would automatically defeat every enemy in Canaan as He had done at Jericho. In addition to being proud and independent, the Israelites failed to wait on the Lord. If Joshua had sought God's face prior to the battle, undoubtedly God would have revealed to him that sin was present in the camp.

The Battle of Ai (vv. 4-5)

As readers, we have already been told that the Lord was burning with anger against Israel, but neither Joshua nor the people knew that. God allowed them to come to the place where they realized that the sin among them would stall any further progress in their invasion of the land. Joshua opted to send three thousand soldiers to attack Ai. The report of the battle is brief. "They fled before the men of Ai." In their retreat they fled to "Shebarim," meaning "quarries." On the descent, thirty-six of the Israelite soldiers who were running for their lives stumbled down the wadi, were struck down, and killed. Though the battle was not a large one, and the number of those killed was relatively small, it was a most significant defeat for Joshua, creating gloom and a sense of doom among the whole company, because the Canaanites would now see that they were vulnerable.

A most important lesson about spiritual warfare can be learned here. We never need to be more careful about defeat than in the flush of victory. The Israelites had the Law written by Moses and the ark of the covenant, which symbolized God's presence. They had just experienced God's power in their victory at Jericho. But they had now unexpectedly experienced a humiliating defeat. When we think we stand the tallest, we need to take heed, lest we fall.

After the defeat came discouragement, for the "hearts of the people melted like water." The imagery of "melting hearts" used here of the Israelites is the same as Rahab used to describe the Canaanites reaction when they had heard how Yahweh had fought for Israel (2:11; 5:1). There was hidden sin in Israel, but most of them did not yet know it. All of them, therefore, suffered defeat and discouragement from this one man's hidden sin.

Joshua's Lament (vv. 6-9)

Joshua did the right thing in response to Israel's defeat: he cast himself before the Lord. Many view him as venting his bitterness and making some wrong assumptions about God, but it is better to see Joshua as perplexed, despondent, and searching for answers. He still trusted in God but could not make sense of the circumstances. "Then Joshua tore his clothes, and fell to the earth on his face before the ark of the LORD until evening, both he and the elders of Israel" (v. 6). Tearing his clothes was a mark of grief, and prostrating himself showed his humility and sense of helplessness. Whatever his frustration, he was in the right place—before the ark of God's presence. The elders of the nation joined him there in these actions and put dust on their heads as mourners. The ark was central in their crossing of the Jordan and in their victory at Jericho. In this chapter it figures once again as Joshua looks for the reason for their defeat. It is always right to be in the presence of God, whether in victory or in defeat.

Joshua questioned why God had brought Israel across the Jordan only to experience defeat at the hands of the Amorites. He also said, "O, that we had been content, and dwelt on the other side of the Jordan!" (v. 7). He failed to take into account that Jericho had been defeated on *this* side of the Jordan. He forgot that God had promised that He would be with him and that no one would be able to stand before him all the days of his life (1:5). Joshua was not complaining in unbelief; he was struggling with his faith and being open with God. In his lament Joshua used the name "Lord GOD" (Sovereign Lord), a compound name for God that indicates the worshipper's deep respect for His power and faithfulness to His promises (v.7). This name occurs some three hundred times in the Old Testament, often when the worshipper is perplexed (cf. Jer. 1:6 and Jer. 32:17).

Frustrated, Joshua proclaimed, "What shall I say when Israel turns its back [literally, "neck"] before its enemies?" (v. 8). This phrase, unique in the Old Testament, captures Joshua's immense frustration. He was concerned for the safety and morale of the Israelites, but he was equally concerned for the Lord's reputation (v. 9). The Israelites were God's chosen people, and if they were defeated it would indicate to the Canaanites that He was unable to protect them. Joshua's argument contended that if the name of the Israelites was cut off from the earth, it would reflect on the name and reputation of their God among other peoples. So he questioned, "Then what will You do for Your great name?" (v. 9). He was concerned for God's name among the pagan Canaanites.

What he did not realize was that God's name had been dishonored within his own ranks.

God Rebukes Joshua (vv. 10–12)

God responded to Joshua's frustration by rebuking him. Joshua knew that God was holy. He also knew that God was powerful: he had experienced God's power firsthand at the Jordan and at Jericho, as well as in Egypt and the wilderness. Therefore, when the Israelites were defeated at Ai, he should have known that something was wrong in Israel. God rebuked Joshua because He was angry about their national sin (v. 1). God did not probe Joshua more deeply to ask him how he felt, nor did he comfort him in his misery. He proclaimed to him, in effect, "This is no time to fall on your face and complain. This is a time for action, and you have failed to take it." What God actually said was: "Get up! Why do you lie thus on your face?" (v. 10).

God spoke plainly to Joshua. "Israel has sinned, and they have also transgressed My covenant which I commanded them" (v. 11). Their present calamity was not due to God letting them down, but because they had sinned. Their sin was explained as a transgression of the covenant. When they broke the covenant they would suffer consequences. The covenant was broken when Achan took what belonged to the Lord, and the camp of Israel was, therefore, accursed (6:18-19). At this point in time, no one but Achan's family knew exactly what had happened, but everyone in the camp should have known that *something* had happened. It was, thus, a hidden sin, but it made all the difference between the triumph at Jericho and the defeat at Ai. Hidden sin has the potential to cause equally damaging results in any congregation of God's people today.

God Describes the Sin (vv. 11-12)

God went on to tell Joshua: "They have even taken some of the accursed things, and have both stolen and deceived; and they have also put it among their own stuff." In the first part of verse 11 God used the words "sinned" and "transgressed." Even though it was all done by one man, God viewed it as a corporate sin. We might summarize their sin this way: first, by taking pride in thinking that they had taken Jericho in their own strength, they underestimated the strength of the enemy at Ai. Second, by presuming that God's presence would follow them no matter what their heart condition, they failed to focus on the ark or to seek God's presence in connection with the battle of Ai. Third, represented by Achan, they had disobeyed when they took the accursed things and broken their covenant with God.

God continued by informing Joshua that the result of Israel's sin was not only that they could not stand before their enemies, but that they would turn their backs ("necks") before them (v. 12; cf. v. 8). Literally, they would flee from them as they had done at Ai. Moreover the effective presence of God would be withheld until the sin was put right by removing "the accursed thing in your midst" (v. 13). God's holy standards could not be compromised. Later in Israel's history God's presence (symbolized by their enemies' capture of the ark) was withdrawn from them with terrible consequences (cf. 1 Sam. 4:21-22).

God Gives Instructions for Restoration (vv. 13–15)

God proceeded to provide Joshua with a recipe for restoration. He repeated the command to rise up, that is, to act immediately (cf. v. 10). The first thing Joshua needed to do was to command the people to sanctify themselves to prepare for what would take place the next day. We should note that all the people were to search their hearts because all of them were considered to be guilty, to some extent, of faithlessness and pride.

The second thing Israel needed to do was to find and remove the accursed thing in their midst (v. 13). To do this they needed to identify the culprit, so God instructed them how to find him. They had to follow a process of determining his tribe first, then his family, then his household, arriving finally at the individual himself. The specific means by which these identifications were to be made is not stated in the text. It may have been done by casting lots, a common custom in Old Testament times (Prov. 16:33). It is possible that the culprit may have been identified by the use of the "Urim and Thummim" stones on the garment of the high priest (v. 14; cf. Num. 27:21).

God went on to explain to Joshua that the culprit, when identified, was to be "burned with fire, he and all that he has" (v. 15). The medieval church used this verse to justify burning at the stake those whom they decided were heretics. Many godly believers suffered unjustly from this terrible form of judgment. In Joshua's case the Lord told him the reason for the harsh judgment. It was because "he has transgressed the covenant of the LORD, and because he has done a disgraceful thing in Israel."

Achan is Identified (vv. 16–19)

Early the next morning Joshua began to do exactly as God had instructed him (vv. 16-18). The tribe of Israel that was "taken" (literally, "snatched") was the tribe of Judah. From the clans of Judah the clan of Zerah was taken. From the clan of Zerah the family of Zabdi was taken. The family of Zabdi was made to come near, and finally the single culprit was identified. It was Achan. This lengthy process was used to stress the seriousness of the situation and the accuracy of God's judgment process. During the entire time it appears that Achan remained silent.

Joshua urged Achan to give glory to God and to tell him what he had done (v. 19). In this instance, glorifying God does not mean praising or worshiping Him; Achan's confession of the truth would bring God glory because it would vindicate God's holy and perfect standard.

Achan Confesses His Sins (vv. 20-23)

Achan confessed right away that he was guilty of sinning "against the LORD God of Israel" (v. 20). God is most certainly glorified when the sins of believers are confessed and immediately dealt with. Personal holiness is of major concern to God. Achan could have identified himself as the culprit and would, perhaps, have been shown some mercy, but he did not. Only when he was singled out did he confess his sin. By then it was too late. He finally spoke up and explained the details of what he had done and where the stolen goods were hidden (v. 21). Although Achan made a full and honest confession of his guilt, he displayed no evidence of repentance. Four personal actions summarize how temptation gave rise to his sin (cf. James 1:14-15):

- ➤ *"I saw."* Achan saw a beautiful cloak from Babylon, two hundred shekels of silver and a bar of gold weighing fifty shekels. He had not sinned at this point, because being tempted is not a sin.
- ➤ *"I coveted."* Achan took the next downward step by lusting after those things. He thereby broke the ninth commandment, "You shall not covet" and, by setting material goods above his pledge to keep God's Law, he also broke the first commandment, "You shall have no other gods before Me."
- ➤ *"[I] took them."* What he coveted, he then stole, and in so doing broke the eighth commandment, "You shall not steal" as well.
- ➤ *"And there they are, hidden."* One sin inevitably leads to another, and in hiding the goods he practiced deception.

The incident is reminiscent of Eve's sin in the Garden of Eden. She *saw;* she *coveted* what she found to be delightful and desirable; she *took* from its fruit, ate of it, and gave it to her husband (Gen. 3:6); then both of them, like Achan, tried to *hide* from God's sight.

Joshua immediately set about to confirm Achan's story, and his messengers found the robe, the silver, and the gold buried beneath the floor of Achan's tent, just as he had said. They brought the stolen items back to Joshua and "laid them out before the LORD" (v. 23). Everyone could see them, but more importantly, the things that were "doomed by the LORD" were brought back to Him to do with as He saw fit.

Achan is Punished (vv. 24-25)

Achan had stolen and possessed what was "devoted"; he was now contaminated and condemned. His sons and daughters were executed with him, so it would appear that they were guilty of helping in the cover up. (Achan's wife is not mentioned. She may not have been part of the cover-up, or Achan may have been a widower.) All his family plus his domestic animals, his belongings, and the things he had stolen were taken out to the Valley of Achor.

Joshua said, "Why have you troubled us? The LORD will trouble you this day." Before the battle of Jericho Joshua had warned the people that if anyone took any of the accursed articles, they would make the camp accursed and bring "trouble" on it (6:18). Joshua uses the same word here. Notice that "all Israel stoned him." The whole nation needed to identify with God's judgment of Achan and did so by being present at and, to some degree, participating in, his execution.

The Memorial Heap of Stones (v. 26)

Achan and his household were stoned to death there in the Valley of Achor, and their bodies were burned along with the stolen items. Achan had been corrupted by the Canaanite things that God had devoted to destruction. Therefore, he was judged like a Canaanite. A large pile of stones was heaped up over them all as a memorial to the future generations who were to examine themselves in the light of what happened that day. Achan means "troubler" and Achor means "trouble." Thus the troubler was buried under a heap of stones in the valley of trouble.

An interesting sidelight on the Valley of Achor appears in the book of Hosea, where it is predicted to become a "door of hope" (Hos. 2:15). The trouble brought by sin, if confessed and forsaken, can open a door to blessing. Achan's sin was confessed and judged, and in the next chapter we find *hope* realized in victory at Ai.

In Conclusion

The great lesson for Israel in this chapter was that God is holy. He hates sin. God cannot bless His people while sin is unconfessed and unjudged. Because we are a body, the sin of one affects the whole. The New Testament church, like Israel in the Old Testament, must recognize this if it wants to experience victory and blessing. The story of Ananias and Sapphira in the early church parallels the story of Achan (cf. Acts 5:1-11). Both teach a solemn lesson that the blessing of God on His people must be accompanied by a proper response to God's holiness. The words of Moses to Israel sum this up for us: "For the LORD your God walks in the midst of your camp, to deliver you and give your enemies over to you; therefore your camp shall be holy" (Deut. 23:14).

JOSHUA 8

Victory at Ai

The events of the previous chapter had discouraged the Israelites. It was perhaps the worst thing they had faced since the report received from the majority of the spies in the wilderness when they chose not to believe that God would give them the inheritance in Canaan that He had promised. Now, thirty-eight years later, Israel had entered the land and had established a base camp at Gilgal. They had seen God flatten the walls of Jericho, but because they, in the person of Achan, had "committed a trespass" (7:1), they had lost a battle to a small fortress city of only twelve thousand people and had fled before their army in disarray and confusion.

Achan had been identified as the one who had 'troubled" Israel and been duly executed, but the question now was: would they would be able to recover? Could they actually defeat the army of Ai? Their defeat by Ai was a major setback for them, and it was now harder for them to believe that they could move forward, especially because Ai was not far from the larger city of Bethel, and beyond it were other powerful city-states. It was easy to allow despair and gloom to dominate their thinking.

Joshua himself was no doubt satisfied that the cause of the defeat had been identified and removed, but he knew the Israelites needed to act quickly to regain the momentum of faith that had brought them across the Jordan and played its part in their victory at Jericho. He was fearful for their future, but the Lord stepped in with some strong words of encouragement, a promise about victory over Ai, and instructions on how to attack.

God Encourages Joshua (v. 1)

God began with telling Joshua, "Do not be afraid, nor be dismayed." God's words were designed to eliminate his fears and to encourage him to lead God's people forward with confidence. God had shared the same words with Moses at Kadesh Barnea when Israel had arrived at the southern border of the Promised Land, just before they sent the twelve spies in to reconnoiter (Deut. 1:21). The Lord Jesus Christ heartened His disciples with similar words at the Last Supper, after which He was betrayed and they were left alone to face the discouragement that Christ's trials and crucifixion created. He said: "Let not your heart be troubled, neither let it be afraid" (John 14:27). Believers need to remind themselves of these words every time they are on the verge of taking a new step of faith.

God Instructs Joshua on Battle Strategy (vv. 1-2)

The Lord then instructed Joshua as to how he should proceed to attack Ai. No instructions had been given before the ill-fated first attack. In fact, no reference had been made to God at all (7:1-3), possibly because Joshua had failed to ask for guidance and had moved ahead without consulting God. Now Joshua was listening when God told him to "take all the people of war with you, and arise, go up to Ai." They needed to return to the very place where they had failed so miserably before. No further progress could be made until Ai was taken. We, too, need to return to the place where we stumble in our spiritual lives. We need to gain victory over the sins that we commit before we can make progress. First, God *commanded* Joshua, "Go up to Ai." Then God *promised* him that He had already given Ai into their hands: "the king of Ai, his people, his city, and his land." God's promises always accompany His commands. When the Lord Jesus Christ commissioned His disciples, He commanded them, "Go therefore and make disciples." He then promised them, "I am with you always" (Matt. 28:18-20).

The Lord instructed Joshua: "You shall do to Ai and its king just as you did to Jericho and its king." We do not know from the record of the capture of Jericho in chapter 6 exactly what happened to the king, but we assume from verse 29 of this chapter that he had been hung on a tree. God not only gave them the command to do it; He also promised that they would be successful. In this way God promised Joshua a victory as complete as the one at Jericho. God continued, "Only its spoil and its cattle you shall take as booty for yourselves." They were now free to take all the livestock and useful articles as plunder. They were not, however, to touch the idols or gods. If only Achan had waited until the next battle, he could have had all the plunder he wanted and lived to enjoy the land of blessing! How much we believers forfeit when we become impatient and failed to obey God by submitting to His timing.

Description of the Battle of Ai (vv. 3-26)

The careful reader will discover that it is very difficult to fit every detail into a consistent sequence of events, to figure out the exact timing of each event, or to be sure about the right numbers of people involved in the various aspects of the battle. The difficulties arise because the account provided here is not a strict historical record. Rather, it is a series of scenes presented where some details are repeated and others are added as the author works toward a climax and creates the desired effect on the reader. Joshua has previously used this same technique twice, in regard to the crossing of the Jordan (cf. 3:7-8, 9-13) and the march around Jericho (cf. 6:4-5, 16-20).

For the purpose of this commentary, the view will be taken that the whole army marched from Gilgal to Ai and made camp to the north of the city (vv. 9, 11). From there the ambush detachment of five thousand men slipped into position on the west side of Ai in the dark before the attack (vv. 2, 9, 12), while Joshua went into the valley with his main army of thirty thousand during the night before attacking the city (v. 13). (The difference in the number of men involved in the ambush has been a point of discussion. Verse 3 indicates thirty thousand, while verse 12 says five thousand. Many assume that the number thirty thousand is a copyist's error, for the higher number seems too many to deal with a total population of twelve thousand people in the city.)

On the morning of the battle, Joshua, the elders, and all the people of war pretended to attack the front (east side) of the city (vv. 5, 10). In response, the army of Ai came out to meet them in battle. The Israelites pretended to take fright and retreat eastward, just as they had done the first time (vv. 5, 6, 15). At that moment, Joshua signaled the men of the ambush and they attacked the city from the rear. When they entered the city, they lit a signal fire to let the main army know they were successful and then proceeded to set the entire city on fire (vv. 7, 8, 18, 19). The main army, having seen the signal, turned around and slaughtered Ai's men who were trapped between them and the ambush army (vv. 20, 21). As each section of the story is provided, more details are added. Readers who are interested in the actual deployment and chronological problems of the passage should consult critical commentaries.

The Signal of the Stretched-out Hand (v. 18)

At the crucial point in the battle, the Lord took direct and personal charge of the attack. The main army had pretended to fall back from the east side of the city drawing Ai's army out of the city in pursuit. The ambush detachment was prepared for the signal to attack from the west side. At that moment, the Lord told Joshua, "Stretch out the spear that is in your hand toward Ai, *for I will give it into your hand* . . ." (v. 18, emphasis added). We also learn that Joshua continued to hold out his spear "until he had utterly destroyed all the inhabitants of Ai" (v. 26). The *stretched out hand* symbolizes judgment in the Old Testament. Regarding the coming plagues on Egypt, God had told Moses, "I will stretch out My hand and strike Egypt with all My wonders" (Ex. 3:20). Later, concerning those same plagues He said, "The Egyptians shall know that I am the LORD when I stretch out My hand on Egypt" (Ex. 7:5). Isaiah pronounced the great prophecy of the stretched out hand against the people of Judah. Five times the Lord recounted their sins, and at the close of each it is recorded: "For all this His anger is not turned away, but His hand is stretched out still" (Isa. 5:25; 9:12, 17, 21; 10:4). When God told Joshua to stretch out his hand while holding the spear, He was indicating His judgment on Ai.

This scene brings to mind what Moses did in the wilderness forty years earlier during Israel's defeat of the Amalekites (Ex. 17:8-16) when, as long as

Moses held up his rod, Israel prevailed. Here in the battle with Ai, God told Joshua to take a Moses-like position before his army. His stance would have reminded them of that event in their history (though few would have been old enough at the time to have witnessed it). No doubt it assured them that Joshua was indeed a worthy successor to Moses.

Was Bethel Captured Too? (v. 17)

The mention of the involvement of the larger city of Bethel to the west of Ai is intriguing. (The ambush detachment hid between Bethel and Ai.) This verse indicates that Bethel's soldiers left Bethel to assist the men of Ai in fighting against Joshua. No other reference to a battle at Bethel appears in the book of Joshua, but later on we read that Joshua had slain the king of Bethel (12:16). Many have concluded that Bethel helped Ai against Joshua and was defeated by Joshua at the same time. However, Ai receives all the prominence in this chapter because it was necessary to record the spiritual recovery of the Israelites after their humiliating defeat in the first battle of Ai. That there is not a more explicit record of Bethel's takeover by the Israelites is interesting, because that city later became the spiritual center of the land—for the next three centuries. However that may be, there are a number of spiritual lessons from this battle that should not be missed, either by Joshua's original readers or by readers today.

Lessons Learned

The first lesson has to do with Joshua's obedience to God. He received instructions from God about leading the attack and he carried them out to the letter. When God said to him, "Go up," Joshua arose early in the morning and mustered his people (vv. 1, 10). The initial defeat and subsequent victory at Ai was a milestone in the invasion of Canaan.

Another lesson from this chapter is how the Israelites worked together to carry out the complex battle plan. They showed cooperation and unity, some going with the ambush detachment and others staying with the main group. They carried out their duties with perfect timing so that the victory was won and Ai (perhaps Bethel, too) was taken. We in our local churches should fulfill the assignments we are given. We should cooperate with the programs our church leaders set in place that promote the well-being of our congregations and outreach to the unsaved.

A third and more personal lesson is that the Israelites had to recover lost ground before continuing with the conquest of Canaan. They could not simply by-pass Ai and move on into the land. They had to face their former defeat and trust God to help them win the battle. Recovering lost ground is more difficult than winning new ground. What we lose in a moment of giving in to a temptation may take years to recover.

A fourth lesson has to do with the sobering fact that God's holiness is more important than man's life. The Canaanites at Ai and Bethel had to be destroyed because their cup of iniquity was full; that is, their iniquity had reached the level of evil at which God chose to remove them (vv. 24-26; cf. Gen. 15:16). The holy character of God demanded the righteous destruction of these depraved and pagan peoples (v. 26). Post-modern idealists today deny this truth because they do not understand God's holiness. We may wonder at how "full" the cup of iniquity is in many countries of the world today.

A fifth lesson is that just as Joshua's return to fellowship with God brought victory and blessing to his life, so God waits for our return to Him in order to bring us victory and blessing.

The Complete Victory (vv. 27-29)

Following the destruction of the people of Ai the Israelites moved in to take the booty of the battle. They were permitted to plunder the domestic animals and material goods, but nothing else (v. 27; cf. v. 2). What was not burned by the ambush detachment was now completely burned by Joshua (v. 28; cf. v. 19). Thus Joshua made Ai "a heap forever." Ai was never rebuilt, and its exact location is still not identified with certainty today. The modern Arabic word for *heap* is "tell," which is used to describe the heaped up ruins of many ancient cities that have been built and destroyed a number of times at the same location. There are many such heaps of ruins in the Middle East, such as Tell Hazor, Tell Bethshean, etc.

Joshua took the body of the king of Ai and hung it on a tree until evening (v. 29). This practice was common in ancient times as a sign of victory. At sunset they removed his body to the entrance of the city and piled up a large heap of stones over it that was still identifiable when the book of Joshua was written. The victory at Ai and Bethel marks the end of the first phase of the conquest of Canaan. The Israelites had firmly established themselves in the land by God's power and their own spiritual relationship with God. The crossing of the Jordan and the victories at both Jericho and Ai demonstrate the importance of the holiness of God and the spiritual side of conquest. Later victories in the taking of the land of Canaan are not given nearly as much attention as those at Jericho and Ai.

The Reading of the Law at Mount Ebal (vv. 30-35)

A pause occurs in the campaign to invade Canaan between the end of this first phase and the next, when Joshua would subdue and capture the central city-states. It was a most important time for recommitment to God and His covenant. The people of Israel had established a firm foothold in the center of Canaan. Because God had caused the inhabitants of the land to have a consuming fear of them, the Canaanites seemed reluctant to take the initiative and attack

Israel. This left the entire nation free to go twenty miles north of Ai to Mount Ebal and camp there while they conducted these ceremonies. What happened at Mount Ebal is a central feature of their inheritance in the land.

Many commentators do not believe this event took place at all and that, if it did, it occurred much later in the conquest. They cannot see how the whole congregation of Israel could have encamped in the middle of the land for ceremonial purposes while their enemies surrounded them. But this was not the only "impossible" thing they had experienced since they left Egypt. The God who had caused the Red Sea to part and the walls of Jericho to fall down flat had also caused the hearts of the other Canaanites to melt in fear before the Israelites. God would have no trouble in either frightening or quieting the Canaanite cities while the Israelites worshipped Him there at Mount Ebal. Since God had specifically commanded them to perform this ceremony in this place when they had entered the land, He would have made it possible.

Fulfilling Moses' Command (vv. 30-31)

In worshipping there at Mount Ebal, Israel was carrying out the commands given to them by Moses before he died. At that time they were still on the east side of the Jordan. Moses and the elders had charged them saying, "And it shall be on the day when you cross over Jordan to the land which the LORD your God is giving you, that you shall set up for yourselves large stones, and whitewash them with lime. You shall write on them all the words of this law. . . . On Mount Ebal you shall set up these stones. . . . And there you shall build an altar to the LORD your God, an altar of stones . . . and offer burnt offerings on it to the LORD your God . . . And you shall write very plainly on the stones all the words of this law" (Deut. 27:2-8).

"Then Joshua built an altar to the LORD, the God of Israel in Mount Ebal" (v. 30). Mount Ebal rose above the city of Shechem, which means "shoulder" because it was built on a shoulder between Mount Ebal on the north side and Mount Gerizim on the south. The two mountains are about one and one half miles apart at the top. From the top of Mount Ebal you can see a large part of the land of Canaan in all four directions. Five hundred yards separate them at the bottom. All the Israelites went on this "spiritual pilgrimage" to Mount Ebal for this specific occasion.

It was there at Shechem in the shadow of Mount Ebal that Abraham had built his first altar to the one true God on first entering Canaan. There God had told him that he and his seed (descendants) would inherit this land (Gen. 12:6-7). Now that Abraham's descendants had become a nation and God was giving them the land it was fitting that they gather at that sacred spot and worship God.

The Altar at Mount Ebal (vv. 30-32)

At this crucial point in their national life, several important things happened that are instructive to us today. The first is that Joshua built an altar to the Lord. In obedience to the words of Moses, the altar, like the altar at Sinai, was to be built of uncut stones "over which no man had wielded any iron tool" (cf. Ex. 20:24; Deut. 27:5-6). This is the first altar mentioned in the book of Joshua. Uncut stones may not seem to be nearly as suitable for a constructed altar as cut and squared stones would be, nor would they be as suitable for decoration and design as polished stones. However, when we consider the purpose of the altar and its significance, we discover a lovely picture here. The Old Testament altar was designed as a meeting place between God and man. Holy God and sinful man could only meet at a place where God's holy demands could be satisfied and man's sin could be atoned for. The offerings on the Old Testament altars pictured the coming Savior who would become the one sacrifice for sin forever. Through His sinless sacrifice, sinful man could be forgiven by a holy God.

Jesus came to earth as the lowly son of Mary. His people were looking for a majestic king and failed to recognize God's humble Son, nor did they find anything attractive in Him (Isa. 53:2). The uncut stones on Joshua's altar speak of the Lord Jesus Christ in His perfection. Though He was despised and unattractive to man, to God He was the perfect sacrifice for sin. He lived a sinless life and yielded Himself completely to the Father's will. As no iron tool wielded by man could improve the stones of the altar, so no man could improve God's perfect Servant. Rather, as Moses had indicated, man's tools would only profane the stones (cf. Ex. 20:25). God's Son was "altogether lovely" (Song 5:16).

Having built the altar, Joshua and the people offered burnt offerings and peace offerings on it. This was the second significant event that occurred at Mount Ebal. The Israelites had offered both of these types of offerings when the Law was given at Sinai. Now they offered them again after they had arrived in the land (v. 33; Ex. 20:24; Deut. 27:7).

The *burnt offering* was always to be completely burnt on the altar, resulting in smoke ascending to God as a sweet smelling aroma (Ex. 29:18; Lev. 1: 9-17). It was an offering of pure worship. No one other than God benefited from it, because it pictured Christ pleasing the Father by offering Himself as a perfect offering for sin.

The *peace offering* (or fellowship offering) took account of the people's communion or fellowship with God. Atonement for sin provides for peace with God (Rom. 5:1). The person bringing the offering laid his hand on the head of the animal as he gave it to the priest for slaughter. The priest offered part of it on the altar to God and gave part of it back to the offerer, who roasted it and ate it (Lev. 3:1-17; 7:11-21). Thus, God's people enjoy what God enjoys. Because their sin was atoned for by the blood of the lamb, they now had fellowship with God, pictured by the meat they shared. God gave back to them what they had given to Him.

After the altar of uncut stones had been built and the offerings had been made, the third significant event at Mount Ebal was Joshua writing a copy of the Law of Moses. From Deuteronomy 27:1-8 we assume that a second structure of stones plastered over with lime was erected. It became a written monument, something like the stones known as *steels* on which ancient kings recorded their laws and accomplishments. While the whole congregation watched, Joshua copied "the law of Moses" with a sharp instrument—either the whole sermon of Moses that we know as the book of Deuteronomy or some portion of it.

The Law was written near the altar where the offerings and sacrifices were made. The ark was there as well. Inside the ark were the two tables of the Ten Commandments. Above the tables was the blood-sprinkled mercy seat. The whole scene pictures Christ among His people. First, in the uncut stones of the altar He is pictured as God's Messiah who fully kept His Law. Second, Christ is pictured in the ark of the covenant: as the ultimate sacrifice He kept the Law and, by shedding His blood, atoned for man's sin.

Joshua Reads the Law (vv. 33-35)

When Joshua had finished writing on the lime-covered stone pillar he had erected, half of the people stood on the slopes of Mount Ebal and the other half stood on Mount Gerizim (v. 33). The effect was that they formed a huge natural stadium. Assuming that they followed Moses' directive, the tribes of Reuben, Gad, Asher, Zebulun, Dan and Naphtali stood on Mount Ebal, and the tribes of Simeon, Levi, Judah, Issachar, Joseph (that is, Manasseh and Ephraim), and Benjamin stood on Mount Gerizim (Deut. 27:11-13). Hundreds of thousands of people stood on the two opposite mountains. They looked down on the ark of the covenant, the inscribed pillar, and the smoking altar. It was no doubt one of the most wonderful occasions in the entire history of Israel.

The fourth significant thing that happened there was that the Law was read to everyone. When Joshua had finished writing the Law he read it, "all the words of the law, the blessings and the cursings." Perhaps priests were stationed at intervals up the slopes of the mountains to repeat his words so that all could hear them. When the curses were read the people answered from Mount Ebal with a thunderous "Amen," meaning that they understood and agreed to abide by the warnings. (See Deuteronomy 27:11-26 for Moses' instructions about this.) Then blessings were read in the same manner and the people answered the blessings from Mount Gerizim with another resounding "Amen." Few occasions in the Bible can match the drama of this event.

In Conclusion

God's people were gathered around Him, and they did four things that remind us of the central features of the life of the New Testament church. They offered burnt offerings, which speak of their worship. They offered peace offerings, which speak of their fellowship with one another and with God. They listened to the Law as it was read to them line by line, which foreshadows the early believers continuing in the teachings of sound doctrine. And finally they responded to God by their "amens" in prayer. These same four activities formed the core of the life of the early church and continue to this day among every congregation of true believers, those who devote themselves to "the apostles' doctrine, and fellowship, in the breaking of bread, and in prayers" (Acts 2:42).

JOSHUA 9

The Treaty with Gibeon

Up to this point in the invasion, the Canaanites had been cowering in fear while the children of Israel attacked them, first at Jericho, then at Ai. That scenario now changed (cf. 2:8-11; 5:1) in that they became active in opposition: they began to form coalitions of cities for the purpose of defeating the Israelites. Chapter 9 begins with a gathering of the kings from six different peoples to plan an attack on Israel using their combined armies. Although these kings never actually carried out a single combined strategy, we can observe their change in tactics in opposing Israel's invasion.

The Canaanites Form Alliances against Israel (vv. 1-2)

The Canaanite kings who met to confer about their defensive strategy are described as coming from three geographical areas which are common biblical terms for parts of Canaan—the hill country, the lowlands, and the coast. All three areas stretch from north to south. The hill country consists of the highland area about two thousand feet above sea level that runs north and south of Jerusalem. The lowlands, sometimes called the Shepelah, comprise the somewhat rocky plateau between the hill country and the coastal plain, about one thousand feet in elevation (cf.11:2). Along the coast sits a plain of good farmland stretching from Gaza in the south to Lebanon in the north (cf. 15:12). The widespread areas from which the kings came indicate that united opposition against Israel was growing.

The kings are further described as belonging to six different peoples: Hittites, Amorites, Canaanites, Perizites, Hivites, and Jebusites (cf. 3:10). Many similar lists of the condemned Canaanite nations can be found throughout Scripture, beginning in Genesis 15:18-19. The purpose of those kings meeting together was to oppose Israel in any way they could. From that time until today, 3,500 years later, the nations of the world have opposed God's people whenever they had opportunity. These "gathered together with . . . one accord," literally, with "one mouth."

Fear of the Israelites Diminishes

It may be that when the kings heard that the Israel had been defeated in the first battle at Ai they concluded that Israel's God was not as invincible as they had thought. This rebellion against God and His people is further testimony that their iniquity was full and ready for judgment, as God had said it would be (cf. Gen. 15:16). Actually, their intention to launch a combined attack never came to fruition. Rather than one large alliance, three smaller alliances would attack Israel. The first one was a group of kings in the central part of the land who carried out a subtle plan to trick Joshua into letting them stay in Canaan (Joshua 9). The second alliance was in the southern part of the land (Joshua 10). The third alliance was a coalition of northern kings (Joshua 11).

The Gibeonites Plan to Deceive Israel (v. 3)

The people of Gibeon had heard what Joshua had done to Jericho and to Ai (v. 30). Four cities in central Canaan (Gibeon, Chephirah, Beeroth and Kirjath Jearim [v. 17]) formed an alliance to negotiate a treaty by which they could escape the complete destruction suffered by Jericho and Ai. They evidently knew that the Israelites intended to destroy all the Canaanites and would never agree to an open formal treaty, so they devised a plan to hide their true identity.

Gibeon, the city that led the alliance, was an important city a few miles west of Ai, about six miles northwest of Jerusalem. As well as knowing that Israel was forbidden from making treaties with the people groups of Canaan, they also knew that God *had* said they could make treaties with distant peoples (Ex. 34:11-12; Deut. 20:15-18). How they might have known all this is not revealed. We do know they worked "craftily," so they might have deliberately sent spies to find out.

Worn Out Clothes and Dry Bread (vv. 4-5)

Verses 4 and 5 describe the crafty measures the Gibeonites took to disguise themselves: ". . . old sacks on their donkeys, old wine-skins torn and mended, old and patched sandals on their feet, and old garments on themselves; and all the bread of their provision was dry and moldy."

A Treaty Proposal (vv. 6-8)

The envoys from Gibeon went to the camp at Gilgal to meet with Joshua (v. 6) and said, "We have come from a far country, now therefore make a covenant with us." The men of Israel were skeptical. "Perhaps you dwell among us; so how can we make a covenant with you?" (v. 7). The writer identifies the envoys as Hivites, one of the groups mentioned in the first verse who were plotting against Joshua. The Hivites from Gibeon answered Joshua, "We are your servants." In saying this they were simply being polite, showing respect to them as their hosts. Joshua was still not convinced and asked them further, "Who are you, and where do you come from?" (v. 8). The form of their greeting in verse 6 indicates that they were travelers arriving at their destination, but when Joshua asked where they came from, the verb forms indicate that he thought they were travelers simply passing through. Their deception was working.

Worn Out Travel Gear (vv. 9-13)

The Gibeonites had a full and ready explanation for Joshua's question. They repeated that they had come from a very far country (though they did not name it), mentioning that they had come "because of the name of the LORD your God." In going on to recite the things that Yahweh had done (the miracles in Egypt and the defeat of the two kings beyond Jordan) they were careful to avoid mentioning the recent victories at Jericho and Ai. To have done so would have indicated that they were local people.

The ambassadors from Gibeon went on to say that their elders and all the people of their country had instructed them to take provisions and go to the Israelites. When they met them they were to greet them with great respect and ask to make a covenant with them (v. 11). The Gibeonites showed them their bread which, now stale and crumbled, had been warm and fresh (they lied) when they left home. Their wineskins, now torn, had been new, they said. They showed Joshua their sandals and clothes which, they lied again, had become worn out from their long journey (vv. 12-13). One lie followed another as they wove this deceptive presentation together.

Joshua's Mistake (vv. 14-15)

After listening to the Gibeonites' proposal for peace between their peoples, Joshua and the men of Israel sought to confirm their words by sampling, inspecting, and handling some of their provisions. Having done so, they were satisfied that the visitors were telling them the truth. They trusted their senses. However, they made one serious mistake. The mistake was that "they did not ask counsel of the LORD" (v. 14), despite the fact that God had made provision for Joshua to go to the high priest for direction when Israel wanted to "go out" or to "come in" (Num. 27:18-23). The high priest had some special precious stones on his garment called the Urim and Thummim. When he prayed for the will of God on a matter, the stones would indicate the answer. In the trial of Achan they had sought God's direction and had been specifically guided, but not here. The problem in this situation is not so much that Joshua naively believed the story of the Gibeonites but that he failed to seek the mind of the Lord.

The sin of not asking for God's guidance and direction has been a common one among God's people in every age. Like Joshua we are tempted to rely on our own judgment and wisdom rather than seeking God's. We arrive at our own thought-out conclusions and leave God out of the equation. It is a formula for failure. Solomon exhorted us not to lean on our own understanding (Prov. 3:5) but to have a lifestyle of trusting the Lord and seeking His mind.

The Treaty with the Gibeonites (v. 15)

From what we know, Joshua accepted the Gibeonites' presentation in good faith. Without any further investigation or confirmation of their story he did two things: he made peace with them and he made a covenant with them. The *peace* he made was agreeing to be friends and not go to war with each other. The *covenant* Joshua made was a treaty between them whereby the Israelites guaranteed the Gibeonites' lives. If there were other provisions in the treaty they are not recorded here. The key point that affected what follows was that the Gibeonites obtained the promise from the Israelites that they did not need to fear for their lives.

This covenant promise was presumably extracted from Joshua on the basis that, in being a distant country, the Gibeonites posed no threat to Israel in terms of any defiling influence they could have on them, and that Joshua felt he was within the bounds of God's restrictions (Deut. 20:10-15). The rulers of the congregation of Israel then joined with Joshua and swore an oath to the Gibeonites that they would abide by the terms of the covenant. The "rulers of the congregation" were the chiefs and representatives of the twelve tribes (cf. Num. 1:16).

The Gibeonites' Deception is Discovered (v. 16)

The treaty had barely been concluded when the Israelites discovered that they had been deceived. The "three days" it took to arrive at this conclusion does not need to be three full days, but the third day after the treaty was made. They heard that instead of being from a distant land, the Gibeonites were really close neighbors. Gilgal and Gibeon were less than twenty miles apart. The Gibeonites were actually Hivites, some of the very people that God had told Israel to destroy because of the danger of becoming a snare to them, thereby leading them into idolatry (v. 1; Deut. 7:1-6; 20:16-18). However, Israel was now bound by their oath to keep the covenant, even though they had been deceived. A parallel situation may be cited when Isaac blessed Jacob and could not take it back, even though Jacob and his mother had deceived him into thinking that Jacob was really Esau (Genesis 27).

The Consequences of Carelessness (vv. 17-21)

Another period of three days seems to be indicated in connection with Israel going to talk to the Gibeonites (v. 17; cf. v. 16). It may be that these were two different three-day periods, but it is best to understand that the two verses refer to the same period. The first day was the day the Gibeonites left. Perhaps suspicions arose then about their genuineness. The second day a contingent of Israelites prepared to leave their camp. The third day they traveled to Gibeon and confirmed that they were near neighbors.

Israel acted swiftly. Verse 18 emphasizes the fact that the Israelites did not attack them (v. 18). The entire congregation was angry that Joshua and their rulers had sworn to the Gibeonites "by the LORD the God of Israel" that they would not destroy them (v. 18; cf. v. 15). They only held back from attacking them because of the sworn oath before God. Most likely the reason the Israelites grumbled was because they had lost the opportunity to plunder their cities. The point is that though they wanted to attack the Gibeonites, they did not do so because of the oath. The statement confirms that Joshua "delivered them [the Gibeonites] from the hand of Israel, so they did not kill them" (v. 26).

The leaders assumed full responsibility for making the oath. They had made it in the name of "the LORD the God of Israel," which is emphasized twice (vv. 18-19), and could not therefore violate it. The only thing they could do was to "let them live, lest wrath be upon us" (v. 20)—that is, God's wrath, for breaking their oath.

The Gibeonites Become Woodcutters and Water Carriers (vv. 21-23)

The Israelite rulers came up with a solution to their problem, and God honored it. They would assign the Gibeonite people a servile position among the Israelites. As their servants they would be woodcutters and water carriers for the sacrificial rituals of the tabernacle, and later, the temple. This lowly assignment would effectively prevent them from being in a position to tempt Israel with their idolatry and sinful lifestyle. They would never be allowed to become citizens of Israel. They were given an enormous job requiring very many people and much hard work. Interestingly, two of the Hivite cities had names connected to this work. Beeroth means "wells," and Kirjath Jearim means "city of wood."

When the rulers had made their decision, Joshua called for the Gibeonites. He sharply rebuked them, "Why have you deceived us, saying, 'We are very far from you,' when you dwell near us?" They had acted treacherously, and because of it they were to be cursed. They would always be slaves (v. 23). The Gibeonites would no longer be recognized as a nation in Canaan, nor would they be allies of Israel, but they were to be permanent servants doing very menial work. Although their work connected with the tabernacle would give them opportunity to come to know and believe in the one true God, that is not the point of the story here.

The Hivites explained to Joshua why they had deceived him. They had heard that Yahweh had given the land to Israel and they grew afraid for their own lives. They went on to say, "Here we are, in your hands; do with us as it seems good and right to do to us" (v. 25). They had no choice but to accept the conditions that the Israelites offered. The Israelites were responsible before God to honor their oath. By this judgment Joshua satisfied his angry people and "delivered them out of the hand of the children of Israel, so that they did not kill them" (v. 26).

Joshua adds a concluding summary statement about making the Gibeonites woodcutters and water carriers for the community at large. The latter job would include the service for the "altar of the LORD, in the place which He would choose" (cf. Deut. 12:5), in other words, the place of offerings where the ark resided. At that time "the place" was in Gilgal. Later the ark was placed in Shiloh (18:1), and after that, in Jerusalem by David. Eventually the ark remained in the temple that Solomon built in Jerusalem. The Gibeonites kept serving in this role at least until the day that the book of Joshua was written; "even to this day" (v. 26). There is no hint in Scripture that the Gibeonites ever broke their side of the covenant. Once, under King Saul, the Israelites did break their side of it, and they were subsequently punished (2 Sam. 21:1-9).

In Conclusion

Some helpful lessons for believers may be derived from this chapter. First, we must constantly be on the alert for disguised infiltrators coming into our churches or homes with hidden agendas. Like the Gibeonites they seek their own advantage by compromising the truth. Second, we should learn never to trust our own judgment. Joshua learned this lesson the hard way. Third, we should always take such matters to the Lord in prayer so that our decisions might be influenced by divine wisdom. Fourth we learn that a mistaken decision, like Joshua's, does not mean we are sidelined forever. Joshua's decision to make the Gibeonites woodcutters and water carriers turned out to be a help in the altar worship of the Israelites. God graciously overruled Joshua's error and turned it to His own glory. Fifth, in relation to personal spiritual warfare, this chapter illustrates the fact that Satan is "the father of lies" and we should be alert to his crafty ways of deceiving us as to the seriousness and consequences of sin. The answer is to immerse ourselves in biblical truth and to heed it.

Joshua 10

Victory in the South

Joshua's Israelite troops held a firm foothold in the center of the land—so secure that the entire company of two million Israelites had been able to go to Mount Ebal to re-affirm the covenant (9:30-35). Their enemies in the land of Canaan had been effectively divided in two: one half to the north, the other to the south. Joshua 10 and 11 describe the battle campaigns in which Israel defeated the key Canaanite cities, first in the south then in the north.

When a coalition of kings in the south attacked Gibeon in response to their tricking Israel into making a "deal" with them, Israel had no choice but to honor their treaty and defend Gibeon. In this way, God used that treaty to precipitate the Battle of Gibeon. In the middle of that battle God performed a miracle that precipitated a significant victory for Israel, one that left Joshua and his people in control of the land as far south as Hebron and Eglon. Joshua 10 is the story of this battle and how the Israelites consolidated their power in southern Canaan.

The King of Jerusalem Fears Israel (vv. 1-2)

From the beginning, the Canaanites feared the Israelites. Before they crossed the Jordan, Rahab told the spies that the Canaanites were very fearful of them (2:10-11). When they set foot in the land, the hearts of the Amorites and Canaanites "melted" in fear of them (5:1). The Gibeonites asked for a treaty because they were "much afraid" for their lives (9:24). Then in this passage, the king of Jerusalem, Adoni-Zedek, "feared greatly" because he had "heard how Joshua had taken Ai and had utterly destroyed it—as he had done to Jericho." The fact that the Gibeonites had "made peace with Israel" troubled him especially; Gibeon was a "great city, like one of the royal cities," a strong city by comparison with Ai yet, even though "all its men were mighty," Gibeon had given up without a fight.

Jerusalem is mentioned by name here for the first time in the Bible. It is likely the same city that was called Salem and was ruled by King Melchizedek in the days of Abraham (Gen. 14:18). The names of the two kings have similar meanings. Adoni-zedek means *lord of righteousness,* and Melchizedek means *king of righteousness.* One was an enemy of God and His people; the other was a priest of the Most High God. Their city, Jerusalem, eventually became

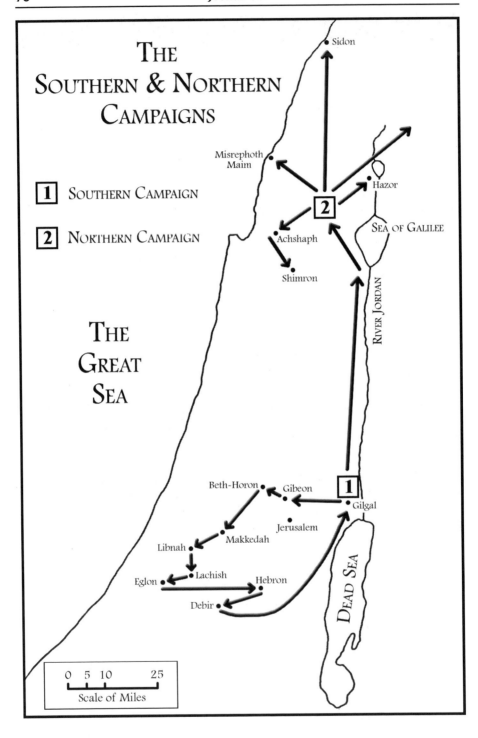

the capital of Israel in the time of David and is destined to be the capital from which Messiah will rule the world.

The Coalition against Gibeon (vv. 3-5)

Adoni-zedek may have thought that the treaty made between Joshua and the Gibeonites was an act of treachery by Gibeon against the other Canaanite cities. Gibeon had broken the "accord" that the kings had made against Israel (cf. 9:1-2). The "great city" (v. 2) of Gibeon was now an ally of Israel and posed a threat to the other Canaanites. Adoni-zedek asked four Canaanite kings to help him in defeating Gibeon and in removing the threat posed by their alliance with Joshua. The kings ruled over four cities south and west of Jerusalem: Hebron, Jarmuth, Lachish, and Eglon. The author calls the reader's attention to the kings' names in particular because they allied themselves against God in the beginning and would all be shamefully hanged in the end. These five kings with their armies gathered together and set up their camp "before Gibeon, and made war against it," that is, they laid siege to the city and attacked (v. 5). Gibeon then sent an urgent message to Joshua to come and defend them.

Israel Comes to Gibeon's Aid (vv. 6-8)

Gibeon's message to Joshua reflected their panic: "Do not forsake your servants; come up to us quickly, save us, and help us, for all the kings of the Amorites who dwell in the mountains have gathered together against us" (v. 6). The terms of their treaty required Israel to come to their aid. But would they come, especially when they had been tricked into making the treaty? This situation became the second test of Israel's faithfulness to the treaty. The first test had occurred when Joshua's own people had wanted to kill the Gibeonites (9:18). This time they might easily have reasoned that God had provided the opportunity for someone else to destroy Gibeon, so they should leave well enough alone. They might have thought that it would have "served them right," but Joshua realized that allowing Gibeon to be destroyed would be a breach of the treaty itself. He therefore acted honorably and responded to the Gibeonites' plea for help.

Joshua and "all the people of war" moved up the valley from Gilgal to fight for the beleaguered city. On their way, the Lord said to Joshua, "Do not fear them, for I have delivered them into your hand; not a man of them shall stand before you" (v. 8). If Joshua had been in any doubt when he had made the decision to honor the treaty with Gibeon, his doubts were soon allayed when God reassured him in this way. God's words to Joshua echoed similar words He had said to him at every crucial point thus far in the campaign: before they crossed the Jordan, before they marched toward Jericho, and before they attacked Ai (1:5; 6:2; 8:1, 18). God once again was encouraging him with these words as Israel marched toward the biggest battle thus far in the invasion.

The Battle at Gibeon (vv. 9-11)

At least twenty miles were traveled from Gilgal to Gibeon. Joshua led his army on a forced march all night and probably reached the besieged city of Gibeon at dawn. Without taking a break, Joshua immediately assailed Gibeon's attackers. The coalition led by Adoni-zedek did not appear to expect any outside help to arrive so quickly, if at all. Having been taken by surprise they were caught in a state of confusion. Before they could organize their defense, the Israelites rushed into their camp and "killed them with a great slaughter at Gibeon" (v. 10). The text, however, does not give credit to Joshua's leadership or to the bravery of his army; instead it credits the Lord with routing the coalition armies before Israel. All the verbs in verse 10 are singular, emphasizing that the Lord alone "routed" them, "killed" them, "chased" them and "struck them down." The author wants us to know that the Lord who gave Israel the land deserved all the credit for winning the battle. Joshua was simply the Lord's general, and the soldiers were the Lord's soldiers.

The coalition forces led by the Adoni-zedek suffered huge losses as the Israelites advanced. They fell back and began to retreat. Their retreat turned into a rout as the coalition panicked and escaped from Gibeon going northwest along the road to Beth Horon, with the Israelites following in hot pursuit. The last line of verse 10 anticipates the end of the battle by telling us that the Israelites continued to strike the enemy as far as Azekah and Makkedah, twenty miles to the south, but in verse 11 the author returns to an earlier event at Beth Horon.

A Severe Hailstorm (v. 11)

With the enemy in full retreat, they reached a place called "the descent of Beth Horon." It was evidently beyond the town where the road turned southwest and descended quickly from the hill country to the lowlands. When the coalition reached this difficult place, "The LORD cast down large hailstones from heaven on them." These hailstones were so large that more of the enemy was killed by the hailstones than by the sword. God had arranged the hailstorm, its timing, and the location, with pinpoint accuracy. It followed the coalition for about twenty miles from Beth Horon to Azekah as they tried to escape southward. The text leaves us with the impression that Joshua's army was not touched at all by the hailstorm. There is no doubt that God fought for the Israelites that day. This was not the only time in which God used hail as an instrument of judgment. See Exodus 9:22-26 and Isaiah 28:2; 30:30; 32:19 for other recorded instances.

Joshua Beseeches the Lord (vv. 12-14)

The narrator takes a third look at the same battle and reports still another remarkable event that happened that day. This time he tells us the sun stood still so that Israel could complete the destruction of the coalition armies (vv. 12-13).

All three elements of this battle are attributed to God. Behind it all was Joshua's prayer: "the LORD heeded the voice of a man; for the LORD fought for Israel" (v. 14).

These remarkable events began with a prayer: "Then Joshua spoke to the LORD" (v. 12). The time is simply stated as "the day when the LORD delivered up the Amorites before the children of Israel." The hour of the day is not mentioned, although the position of the sun and the moon described in verse 12 indicates that it would have been during the early morning in the vicinity of Beth Horon. At that time the sun would be rising to the east over Gibeon and the moon would be setting in the west over Ajalon. Joshua probably prayed before the hailstorm came because the sun and the moon were still visible that morning, but he realized that the enemy was on the run and that it would take time to carry out God's command to destroy them. He most likely requested that God give them time to finish the task. The Greek Septuagint translation of the Scripture agrees with this assumption. Whatever Joshua said, his prayer should be considered in the light of what happened that day and of the summary statement that the "LORD heeded the voice of a man" (v. 14).

The Sun Stands Still (v. 13)

Some discussion among commentators exists as to who "he" is in verse 12: "*He* said in the sight of Israel: 'Sun, stand still over Gibeon'" (emphasis added). Although some translations indicate it was Joshua, the original text is not clear. It may have been Joshua, or it may have been God speaking directly to the sun and the moon. It would appear more likely to be that when Joshua spoke to God, God responded by speaking to the heavenly bodies which then obeyed Him, their Creator, and stopped in their courses. Once again, consider the key phrase in this incident: God was heeding the voice of a man.

The question remains about what actually happened while the Israelites completed the victory (v. 13). Several options have been suggested, none of which are without problems to those who are aware of the magnitude of the scenario created by such a cosmic interruption. Commentators have traditionally believed that the sun and the moon literally stood still from the viewpoint of people on earth. This assumption would, in geological terms, mean that the earth stopped rotating on its axis to make it appear that the sun stood still. Proponents of this *traditional view* simply believe that God performed a miracle and that scientific explanations should not be sought.

A second group believes that some cosmic event such as the tail of a passing comet refracted the sun's light so that there was more daylight in the vicinity of Canaan that day. We might term this the *refracted light view*. Another could be called the *astrological view*, in which proponents think that Joshua asked God for a favorable omen. When the sun and the moon appeared together that morning, he took it as a sign—a good omen—that God would give them the victory. Many modern interpreters take a *figurative view*. They see the poetic language as simply figurative speech, and they rightly point out that the command to the sun and its response are in poetic form, as indicated in many modern translations. To them, the standing still of the sun and moon is merely a figurative description of a great victory.

It is best for us to understand the passage in the traditional way, in that God performed a mighty and inexplicable miracle in response to Joshua's prayer for help (v. 14). We should believe it even though there doesn't seem to be a logical or physical explanation that makes scientific sense. If God could create the universe from nothing, give life to the dust of the ground, and prepare a heaven for His people, He should have had no problem taking care of extra daylight for Joshua and his army. "For with God nothing will be impossible" (Luke 1:37).

The Book of Jasher (v. 13)

The result of Joshua's prayer was that "the sun stood still, and the moon stopped, till the people had revenge upon their enemies." Joshua then explains, "Is this not written in the Book of Jasher? So the sun stood still in the midst of heaven, and did not hasten to go down for about a whole day." The Book of Jasher is an extra-biblical book which has not survived, but it is thought to have been a collection of ancient songs with historical notes. It is mentioned again in 2 Samuel 1:18 and is quoted here to corroborate the great miracle of the longest day. The words "about a whole day" indicate that the day was miraculously lengthened for a number of hours amounting to the length of a day.

The Lord Heeds the Voice of a Man (v. 14)

After stating the facts regarding that remarkable day, Joshua evaluates what happened. It had indeed been a unique day; there has been none like it, either before or since. It was God's answer to an extraordinary prayer. What made Joshua's prayer extraordinary was the stronger than usual wording for how the Lord acceded to his request. The wording is only used three times in the Old Testament: once when Israel prayed for victory over the Canaanites at Hormah (Num. 21:3), here in this passage, and again when Elijah prayed that God would raise up the widow's son (1 Kings 17:22). There was a special urgency in the wording of all three prayers and a special response by God in the way that He answered each of them.

We should also consider that the important truth in this passage is not that the answer to Joshua's prayer was that the sun stood still, but that "the LORD fought for Israel." He did this by routing the enemy before Joshua's army (v. 10), by creating the special hailstorm that destroyed the enemy (v. 11), and by lengthening the day to provide time to complete the battle (v. 13). These three answers to Joshua's prayer made it a day like no other. These truths ought to be an encouragement when we pray in times of great stress, knowing that God will honor our request by listening and responding, sometimes with His miraculous power.

We then read that "Joshua returned and all Israel with him to the camp at Gilgal" (v. 15). These words seem to conclude the Battle of Gibeon, but the alert reader will notice that additional verses continue to add further details of the battle and that the same words are repeated at the end of the chapter. The reason may be that an ancient copyist inserted the verse twice in error, but more probably it was deliberately included twice because it was the intention of the author to close off the two sections with the same concluding words. Both in the Battle of Gibeon (vv. 1-15) and the subsequent conquest of southern Canaan (vv. 28-43) it states that the Lord fought for Israel and that Joshua then returned to his camp (cf. vv. 14-15, 42-43).

The Completion of the Battle of Gibeon (vv. 16-21)

Verses 16 to 21 provide some added detail about the "mop-up campaign" of the battle. The retreating Canaanite forces continued running through the hailstorm toward the south until they came to Azekah. Joshua then received a report that the five kings were holed up together in a cave at Makkedah, about ten miles south of Azekah. Joshua instructed his men to pile up large stones in the mouth of the cave to trap them inside and to post a guard (vv. 16-18).

Joshua, however, would not yet let his men rest. He ordered them to take advantage of the long day and to keep pursuing the enemy before they could reach the safety of the walled cities from which they had come—Jerusalem, Hebron, Jarmuth, Lachish and Eglon. The last two cities, Lachish and Eglon, were quite nearby, so every minute counted. Joshua reminded his men again that, "The LORD your God has delivered them into your hand" (v. 19). In pursuing the enemy, Israel accomplished what is termed a "very great slaughter." Some of the coalition soldiers did, however, reach the safety of their fortified cities (v. 20).

At the end of the day, the people returned to the camp at Makkedah "in peace." Evidently the Israelites had suffered no casualties. Verse 21 says that "no one moved his tongue against any of the children of Israel" (v. 21). This phrase literally means "no one sharpened his tongue," or "no one uttered a word." It means Israel was so safe from attack that the Canaanites would not be able to utter a word, far less mount any opposition. This same phrase was used by God on the night of the slaying of the firstborn in Egypt when He spoke of Israel's protection from the destroying angel. The Egyptians would wail, but among the Israelites not even a dog would bark or "move its tongue" against man or beast (Ex. 11:7). The repeating of the same phrase may have been deliberate to once again make the comparison between Moses and Joshua.

The Symbol of Victory (vv. 22-24)

The story of the five kings concludes with their public execution. Joshua told his men to open the cave where they had been imprisoned and to bring them out. The names of the cities over which the kings ruled are named for a third time so the reader can better appreciate the extent of the victory (v. 23; cf. vv. 3, 5). What began as a threat against Israel in the earlier verses of this chapter had turned into a great victory for them.

In calling for the captains of the army to come forward and put their feet on the necks of the defeated foe, Joshua was practicing a common custom of ancient times. A series of prophecies using this imagery appear in the Scripture relating to the victory of Messiah over His enemy, Satan. The first pictures Him with His foot on the head of the serpent (that is, Satan, Gen. 3:15). Although Satan would bruise His heel, Messiah would crush Satan's head. It points to Christ's victory over Satan at the cross when, through death, He would "destroy him who had the power of death, that is, the devil" (Heb. 2:14). Second, David prophesied of the risen Messiah awaiting His kingdom. He spoke of God saying to Messiah, "Sit at My right hand, till I make Your enemies Your footstool" (Ps. 110:1). Finally, Paul foretold of Christ's victory with the same figurative language: "For He must reign till He has put all enemies under His feet" (1 Cor. 15:25).

Paul applied this principle to the believers in Rome and, by extension, to us. After praising his readers for their obedience he exhorted them, in relation to false teachers, to "be wise in what is good, and simple [innocent] concerning evil." He then comforted them with the prospect that "the God of peace will crush Satan under your feet shortly" (Rom. 16:19-20). We too should live in the light of that promise by holding to the truth and obeying God's Word now.

The Five Kings are Executed (vv. 25-27)

Joshua then said to his men, "Do not be afraid, nor be dismayed, be strong and of good courage, for thus the LORD will do to all your enemies against whom you fight" (v. 25). He encouraged his men with the same words that Moses had first spoken and that had become a keynote of their campaign for Canaan. The phrase "Be strong and of good courage" appears in Deuteronomy 31:6, 7, 23 and in Joshua 1:6, 7, 9, 18; and 10:25. The campaign was far from over, and certainly they needed encouragement along the way. In this same vein, Jesus told His disciples to "be of good cheer," or courage (John 16:3).

Joshua then put the five kings to death and hanged them on five trees until evening (v. 26), just as he had done earlier to the king of Ai (8:29). This form of displaying their dead bodies emphasized the fact that they (and the Canaanite people over whom they had reigned) were cursed by God. Deuteronomy 21:23 says, "He who is hanged is accursed of God." That same verse includes the instruction God gave as to how to dispose of the dead: at sunset, the bodies were to be removed from public display and buried "so that you do not defile the land which the LORD your God is giving you as an inheritance." Joshua fulfilled this command by burying the five kings in the same cave in which they had been imprisoned (v. 28). The army then piled up large stones at the cave's mouth as a lasting memorial to their great victory. It was the third visible memorial they had built in Canaan. The first had been made of stones from the middle of the Jordan River to commemorate the crossing of the Jordan (4:19-24). The second was a heap of stones piled over the body of the slain king of Ai, commemorating their victory over Ai (8:29).

The Completion of the Southern Campaign (vv. 28-39)

Joshua did not include any other detailed descriptions of the battles for Canaan in his book. He simply named those kings and their cities which were vanquished with a few scant details in a kind of summary form. This form becomes the pattern for the remainder of the book of Joshua. They bear testimony that the promises made to Joshua at the beginning of the conquest were fulfilled as one Canaanite city after another was defeated and destroyed. The readers need to keep this in mind throughout the next fourteen chapters. The final verses of chapter 10 are the beginning of this summary report.

We can be confident that this portion of Scripture comprises reliable historical records. They are not, as some have said, simply expressions that stereotype the victories. Similar language is used, however, to describe most of the victories in this section, such as the phrase about those who fought ("Joshua . . . and all Israel") and the phrase about how many were killed ("He left none remaining"). Six of the seven victories are compared to a previous victory, for example, "as he had done to the king of Jericho" (v. 28). Nevertheless, enough variety in the forms of expression exist to assure the reader that these are genuine records and not simply a repetition of stock phrases.

In chapter 10 Joshua mentions seven cities in the south that were captured by Israel: Makkedah, Libnah, Lachish, Horam, Eglon, Hebron, and Debir. Other cities in the area were probably taken at the same time but not reported until later in the book (cf. 12:13-15). The conquest of these southern cities probably took several weeks to accomplish, although the exact number is not indicated. Some of the cities such as Hebron and Debir would require a second effort to subjugate them (see 15:13-14 and 15:15-17). Consulting a map for the geographical location of all the places mentioned throughout the book of Joshua will greatly enhance the reader's comprehension of the book.

In Conclusion

These final verses conclude the section which began in chapter 9 with the treaty with Gibeon and continued through this chapter with the Battle of Gibeon. In verse 40, four regions of the country are mentioned in reference to how

"Joshua conquered all the land." These regions include the mountain (hill) country, the south, the lowland, and the wilderness slopes. The hill country and the lowlands have been noted before (9:1-2). The south had just been conquered, but what the slopes refer to is not known for certain. In these areas, Joshua "utterly destroyed all that breathed," just as he had been commanded. Verse 40 also lists the extremities of the land Joshua had thus far captured—from Kadesh in the southwest to Gaza on the west, and from Goshen (probably southwest of Hebron), to Gibeon in the central highlands. These geographical limits may indicate that other cities were captured beside those mentioned in this chapter.

The summary statement also reminds us that "the Lord God of Israel fought for Israel" (v. 42). The central idea that it was God, not Joshua, who gave them the land, must not be missed. With the southern campaign behind them, Joshua and all Israel returned to their base camp at Gilgal (v. 43).

Joshua 11

The Northern Campaign and Final Victory

The final phase of the Israelite invasion of Canaan was a campaign in the northern part of the land. It contains some striking similarities to the southern campaign. Both were responses to attacks initiated by a leading Canaanite king in that area. Both kings feared the Israelites' advance and formed a coalition with other city-states to try to stop it. The records of the two battles both begin with the phrase, "It came to pass when . . ." (10:1; 11:1). In both campaigns Joshua won a decisive battle in the beginning which was followed by further military engagements to increase their control in the land.

The Northern Coalition (vv. 1-5)

The leader of the northern coalition was Jabin, king of Hazor, a city about ten miles north of the Sea of Galilee that was strategically situated on the main caravan route from Egypt to Damascus. According to scholars, the population of Hazor was about 40,000. Hazor appears in later portions of Scripture (Judg. 4:2; 1 Sam. 12:9; 1 Kings 9:15; etc.). A King Jabin is mentioned in the reference to Hazor in Judges (in the period following Joshua's death), but he is obviously not the same Jabin as the one in this chapter. This King Jabin had heard of Joshua's exploits in the south and determined to gather together a larger coalition to defeat him. He called the kings of Madon, Shimron, and Achshaph to join him in going to battle against Israel (v. 1). Madon was probably located to the west of the Sea of Galilee, and Shimron and Achshaph in the Valley of Jezreel.

Regions and Peoples

In the forming of the coalition, the *cities* are listed in the first verse, the *regions* in the second, and the *peoples* in the third verse. The four regions mentioned in verse 2 are the "mountains" to the north toward Mount Hermon; the "plain" or valley south of "Chinneroth" (Galilee), which is the valley of the Jordan; the "lowlands," which were the foothills to the west; and the "heights of Dor," which may refer to the foothills east of the port city of Dor.

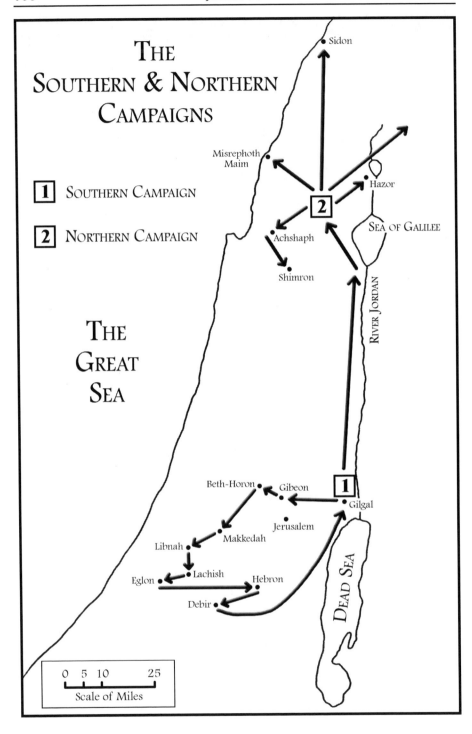

The six peoples listed in verse 3 are the same as those who gathered against Joshua before the Battle of Gibeon (9:1): the Canaanites, the Amorites, the Hittites, the Perizzites, the Jebusites, and the Hivites. The Hivites mentioned here are connected with Mount Hermon and the land of Mizpah, one of four places in the Bible with that name. It is possible that the writer's intention was to include the same six peoples in the context of both the northern and the southern campaigns. Notice that these people groups obviously did not segregate themselves into their own areas, but congregated in pockets throughout the land.

Preparations for the Battle of Merom (vv. 4-5)

The coalition gathered at the waters of Merom, which is usually identified with Lake Huleh a few miles north of the Sea of Galilee and not far from Hazor. The enemy's strength was "as the sand that is on the seashore in multitude, with very many horses and chariots." Horses and chariots are mentioned as a substantial part of their weaponry. The first biblical reference to these means of warfare was when Pharaoh and the Egyptians pursued the Israelites during their exodus (Ex. 14:7-28). Joshua, of course, had nothing to match them. To him, the amassed armies and their chariots would have appeared as the most formidable foe he had faced thus far.

The Battle of Merom (vv. 6-9)

While King Jabin had been assembling the northern coalition, Joshua appears to have moved his army northward to the area of Galilee. Between the defeat of the southern coalition and this battle other battles likely occurred of which there is no biblical record. For example, we can assume cities like Taanach and Megiddo (mentioned in 12:21) were probably taken before the battle of Merom. Joshua went on the offensive as he approached the northern coalition near Merom. As he did so, the Lord told Joshua not to fear; within twenty-four hours He would deliver the enemy "slain before Israel" (v. 6). He instructed Joshua to hamstring the horses and burn the chariots.

The hamstringing of the horses was intended to make them unusable as warhorses while preserving them for domestic purposes. More than four hundred years later, David followed the same directive (2 Sam. 8:4). The Lord had cautioned the Israelites through Moses that they were not to multiply horses for the purpose of war as the Egyptians had done (Deut. 17:16). In relation to burning the chariots, in all probability the chariots were largely made of wood (except for axles and possibly wheel hubs, which were likely made of iron). The purpose of destroying the chariots and making the horses unfit for battle was to help Israel to simply rely on the Lord. Many years later David expressed this idea in the Psalms: "Some trust in chariots, and some in horses; but we will remember the name of the Lord our God" (Ps. 20:7).

When Joshua attacked the forces united by Jabin, "The LORD delivered them into the hand of Israel" (v. 8). As we have noted in the records of former battles, the point stressed is that it was God's power—not Joshua's strategy or the skill of his men—that gave them the victory. The Israelite army chased the coalition in several directions: as far west as Greater Sidon on the coast, to the Brook Misrephoth to the south of Sidon, and eastward to Mizpah near Mount Hermon. The battle was a complete victory for Israel in that it says, "They left none of them remaining" (v. 8; cf. 10:28, 30, 33 etc.). Joshua obeyed God's instructions in hamstringing the horses and burning the chariots (v. 9). He and his army's faithfulness continued as a consistent feature as they advanced into Canaan (cf. 10:40).

The Completion of the Northern Campaign (vv. 10-15)

Just as the record of the southern campaign added more details about what happened in the wake of the first and decisive battle at Gibeon, here too we learn more details about what happened after the battle at Merom (cf. 10:28-39). The period of time it took and the sequence of events is not always clear. We read, "Joshua turned back . . . and took Hazor, and struck its king with the edge of the sword." Hazor is recorded as being "the head of all those kingdoms," but Joshua defeated it. When he was finished, "There was none left breathing" (v. 11).

Hazor was one of just three cities that Joshua and the Israelites are recorded as having burned to the ground. They were Jericho, Ai, and Hazor. At Jericho the curse was most complete in that it included cattle, people, and goods (6:21). At Ai the Israelites were allowed to keep the cattle and the booty (8:2, 27). In the other cities in the north, Joshua attacked and killed the inhabitants but kept the spoils, just as Moses had commanded (v. 14; cf. Deut. 20:10-18; Num. 33:50-53).

The section closes with another summary statement of Joshua's obedience to the explicit commands God had given to Moses regarding how the Israelites were to treat the cities, peoples, domestic animals, and goods of Canaan. He "left nothing undone of all that the LORD had commanded Moses" (v. 15) and heeded well the commands that God gave him before the conquest: "Do according to all the law which Moses My servant commanded you" (1:7).

A Summary of the Southern and Northern Campaigns (vv. 16-17a)

By this time the Israelites were in control of the major areas of Canaan. First the thrust into Ai, Bethel, and Mount Ebal provided them a strong position in the center of the land. Second, the defeat of the southern coalition and the pursuit of the five kings as far as Hebron subdued the southern part of the land. Finally, the campaign against the coalition of Hazor and its allies gave them control of the north from Mount Hermon to the Mediterranean coast. Many pockets of resistance and unconquered towns remained, but the children of

Israel now dominated the land, creating a very different scenario to the tenuous situations experienced by Abraham, Isaac, and Jacob, who had to gain and maintain the favor of the local inhabitants to be able to live there.

Seven Regions Conquered

Joshua begins his summary by mentioning seven regions where significant victories had been won (v. 16). Four of these regions were also listed in the summary of 10:40-41: the *mountain country* or hill country of Judah; the *south*, sometimes called the Negev in southern Judah; the *lowland* called the Shepalah; *Goshen*, probably a town and area southwest of Hebron (cf.10:41) (not the Goshen in Egypt, of course). Three other regions are listed which were not mentioned in chapter 10: the "Jordan plain," or *arabah*, the rift valley where the Jordan flows; the *mountains of Israel*, or hill country of Israel, referring to the central highland area, as distinct from the hill country of Judah around Jerusalem; and the *lowlands* which lie between the mountains and the coastal plain.

Northern and Southern Extremities

The northern and southern borders of the conquered land clearly indicate the extent of Joshua's conquest (v. 17). The southern extremity was "Mount Halak and the ascent to Seir," which is probably the same as the modern *Jebel Halaq*, a low mountain ridge on the western side of the Arabah from which Mount Seir may be seen on the eastern side. It is east of Kadesh Barnea, as mentioned in 10:41. The northern extremity is given as "Baal Gad in the Valley of Lebanon," a reference to the valley between the two north/south ranges in Lebanon today.

The Length of the Canaanite Conquest (vv. 17b-18)

The end of verse 17 speaks of Joshua having captured all Canaan's kings and striking them down, while verse 18 speaks of Joshua making war a "long time" with them. The war took longer than we might assume from a casual reading of this first half of the book. The "long time," literally "many days," is an extended period. The references to time in Joshua are rather vague, so we do well to recognize that the campaign for Canaan took years, not weeks, to accomplish. Caleb states that it was forty-five years from the time that he reported as one of the twelve spies until the time he captured Hebron (14:10-12). If the Israelites wandered thirty-eight years in the wilderness after the spies' report in Kadesh Barnea (Deut. 2:14), then the conquest of Canaan took about seven years.

God's Activity in the Conquest (vv. 19-20)

Apart from Gibeon's achieving peace with Israel by subterfuge (chapter 9), no other city tried to do so, as it is recorded that "all the others they took in battle." According to verse 20, the Canaanites did not try to negotiate a peace because God had hardened their hearts to the point where they stubbornly fought against Israel to the end. Their hardness of heart led to their destruction, which was exactly as God had intended and as Moses had commanded (Deut. 20:16-18).

God Hardens Their Hearts

The question then arises, if God hardened the Canaanites' hearts, was it fair for the Israelites to destroy them? Several factors are involved here. The first relates to God Himself. Psalm 7:11 says, "God is a just judge, and God is angry with the wicked every day." Psalm 11:5 says, "The wicked and the one who loves violence His soul hates." God's purity and holiness demand that all wickedness be judged. The Canaanites were a wicked people whose cup of iniquity had been filling for hundreds of years (Gen. 15:16). Just as a cup can only contain so much liquid, so the Canaanites' "cup" of evil was filled to the brim. They could not get any worse. As a people, God destined them for destruction. The Canaanites had revolted against God and chosen a path of iniquity. They did not repent when they heard of God's favor towards Israel and His miracles on their behalf. Therefore, God hardened their hearts to fight against His people, thus precipitating their downfall.

God did the same thing to Pharaoh in Egypt under very similar circumstances. Pharaoh had defied God when he declared, "Who is the LORD, that I should obey His voice to let Israel go? I do not know the LORD, nor will I let Israel go" (Ex. 5:2). God therefore taught Pharaoh that He was a God to be feared by bringing about a series of plagues (Ex. 7:5; 8:10). God hardened Pharaoh's heart as one plague after another descended on the people of Egypt. On the night of the Passover the Lord had spoken to Moses and Aaron of the work of the destroying angel, saying, "Against all the gods of Egypt I will execute judgment: I am the LORD" (Ex. 12:12). In Pharaoh's case, he had defied God and had hardened his own heart before God hardened his heart to receive judgment. In much the same way the Canaanite kings had defied God and hardened their own hearts. As a result, God further hardened their hearts against the Israelites, and through Moses He commanded the Israelites to utterly destroy them (Deut. 20:16). The example of Rahab the harlot shows that it was possible for individuals to repent of their evil ways, turn to the Lord, and be accepted.

The Anakim (vv. 21-22)

The final military engagement recorded concerns the destruction of the Anakim. As with several other battles, the only reference to any time sequence is by the phrase, "at that time." We do not know the exact point in the seven-year conquest when these events occurred. The writer probably included it here as a fitting conclusion and climax to the account of the conquest. The reader will recall that when the ten spies had seen the walls of the cities and the sons of Anak that their hearts had melted for fear (Num. 13:28; Deut. 1:28), for they had heard the saying, "Who can stand before the descendants of Anak?" (Deut. 9:2). They reported to the people, "We saw the giants . . . and we were like grasshoppers in our own sight, and so we were in their sight" (Num. 13:33). It was due to the ten spies' fear of the giants that the people refused to enter the land. Now, with the story of the conquest of the land nearly complete, Joshua ties the events together by recording the defeat of the Anakim.

Who were the Anakim? They were the descendants of Anak. Anak's father was Arba after whom the town of Kirjath-Arba, later known as Hebron, was named. Three particular descendants of Anak occupied Kirjath-Arba and were driven out by Caleb (15:13-14). As previously mentioned they were described as "giants" (Heb. *Nephilim,* meaning "fallen ones," Num. 13:33). They are also referred to in Genesis 6:4 as the progeny of the sons of God (fallen angels) and the daughters of men (human females). These giants were "mighty men" who used their power pursuing wicked ends. Some scholars say they were all destroyed in the flood, but in Genesis 6:4 Moses says that they lived in the days of the flood *"and also afterward."*

In this summary statement we are told that "Joshua cut off the Anakim," which means that he completely eliminated them from the area, bringing about God's judgment on them because their wickedness was full. By the time he was finished, the only places where the Anakim still existed were in three Philistine cities, Gaza, Gath and Ashdod, all outside the conquered area (v. 22). We read of the Anakim again in Scripture when David challenges Goliath, the giant of Gath (1 Samuel 17). God empowers us too to defeat the giants in our lives, like fear and doubt.

In Conclusion

The summary statement for this section is the last verse of the chapter, verse 23: "So Joshua took the whole land, according to all that the LORD had said to Moses; and Joshua gave it as an inheritance to Israel according to their divisions by their tribes. Then the land rested from war." Pockets of resistance and areas where Canaanites still lived remained, but Joshua had subdued the major cities and was in control of the whole land. There was no longer any need for the entire army to attack major targets en mass, so each tribe would be responsible for the area they would be assigned. This summary statement links the three main ideas at the beginning of the book of Joshua:

- ➢ *Joshua's obedience* in carrying out all that the Lord had commanded Moses to do (1:7)
- ➢ *The people's inheritance* in the land, which God had promised (1:3-6)
- ➢ *The land's rest* from the evil of the Canaanites and the war to exterminate them (1:13, 15).

This verse also anticipates the remainder of the book of Joshua regarding how the land would be divided. The theme of rest which was first mentioned in 1:13 and 15 is mentioned several more times in Joshua (14:15; 21:44; 23:1). The writer of Hebrews uses the theme of physical and political rest in the conquered land, fragile as it was, as an illustration of the spiritual rest into which the believer can come by faith (Heb. 4:11).

JOSHUA 12

Conquered Kings and Cities

Joshua 12 enumerates thirty-three kings whose armies and territories were defeated by the Israelites during the conquest. It serves as an appendix to the first eleven chapters to summarize the cities and regions over which Israel gained control. These areas were on both sides of the Jordan taken under the leadership of Moses and Joshua, and they were given to the twelve tribes as a *possession* (12:1, 7). Joshua humbly counted up these victories in order to give God the glory.

Joshua's record is divided into two parts. He first lists the two kings and their territories which Moses had defeated east of the Jordan. He then lists thirty-one kings and their cities on the west side of Jordan who were defeated after God had appointed him to lead His people. The point emphasized is that the kings were *defeated* and the lands were *possessed* (vv. 1, 7).

The Possession of Land East of Jordan (vv. 1-2)

The extent of their possession on the "other side of the Jordan toward the rising of the sun" is described in the first verse from its southern extremity to the northern extremity. The River Arnon, the southern border of the land, flows west into the center of the Dead Sea. From there the land stretched northward to Mount Hermon and included all the "plain" or valley on the east of Jordan.

In verses 2 through 5 Joshua describes the names and the lands of the kings who ruled the area east of Jordan and were defeated by Moses. Moses himself provides an excellent description of those battles in Deuteronomy 2:32–3:17 (see also Num. 21:21-35). These lands had been claimed and settled by the tribes of Reuben, Gad, and half of the tribe of Manasseh before the Israelites had crossed the Jordan. Now that the campaign on the west side had been concluded and they had fulfilled their obligation, they were able to return to their families in the east. Joshua includes their lands as part of the catalog of conquered territories that now made up the land of Israel.

The Southern Section of TransJordan (vv. 3-4)

The land east of the Jordan consisted of two major sections, one to the south and one on the north. The southern section had been ruled by Sihon, king of the Amorites, from Heshbon, a site not far from modern day Amman, Jordan. His kingdom stretched from the city of Aroer on the Arnon River in the south, northward to the River Jabbok which flows into the Jordan about half way between the Dead Sea and the Sea of Galilee. In the Jordan Valley his territory extended farther north to the sea of Chinneroth (Galilee). From that point Sihon's land reached southward through the Arabah (Jordan Valley) to the "Salt Sea" (Dead Sea) and continued on "below the slopes of Pisgah." From that area Moses had been allowed to see the Promised Land (Deut. 34:1).

The Northern Section of TransJordan (vv. 4-6)

The northern section of the land east of the Jordan had been ruled by Og king of Bashan. Og was "of the remnant of the giants" or Rephaim (cf. Deut. 3:11). Rephaim were already in the land and were living in Ashteroth Karnaim when Abraham settled there (Gen. 14:5), but God promised Abraham that his seed would be given the land of the Rephaim (Gen. 15:18-20). Like the Anakim (11:21), they were of great stature and seem to have descended from the Nephilim (Deut. 3:11). Like the Anakim, they were destined to be destroyed. Og's kingdom was generally north of the Jabbok River and east and northeast of the Sea of Chinneroth as far as Mount Hermon. While the description is not as clear as that of King Sihon in the south, it appears that part of Gilead and all of what we know as Bashan was included. The Geshurites and the Maachathites lived northeast of the Sea of Chinneroth and were not subdued by the Israelites (Deut. 3:14; Josh. 13:13).

The Possession of the Land West of Jordan (vv. 7-24)

The second half of the chapter deals with the kings and their lands on the west side of the Jordan that Joshua conquered. Again the emphasis is on the *possession* of the land (cf. vv. 1, 7). For a third time Joshua summarizes and describes the lands taken in the invasion (vv. 7-8; cf. 10:40; 11:16-17), completing his summary with a list of thirty-one conquered cities that were ruled by kings (vv. 9-24).

Areas and Peoples

This summary of the boundary lines is similar to the one in 11:17 because the tribes are given their land *according to their divisions*. It differs from that one in that it begins in the north with the city of Baal Gad and ends in the south with "Mount Halak and the ascent to Seir." Both summaries look back to the conquest and forward to the division of the land. After the description of the boundary lines (v. 7) six geographical areas are described and six people groups are named (v. 8). The geographical areas are the same ones mentioned in the first eleven chapters, and the six peoples as the ones given in 3:10.

Thirty-one Kings and Cities

In the summary Joshua mentions several clusters of cities ruled by kings. He begins with the first two primary cities conquered by Israel, Jericho, and Ai (v. 9). Then he mentions a cluster of thirteen cities in the south (vv. 10-16a), followed by a cluster of five cities in the center of the land (vv. 16b–18). He concludes with a cluster of eleven cities in the north (vv. 19-24). Five of them were the original southern coalition against Joshua (10:3, 23). Gezer and Debir are mentioned in 10:33 and 38. Three of the others have not been mentioned earlier in the book of Joshua: Geder, Hormah, and Arad. Geder's location is unknown. Hormah and Arad are in the Beersheba area (cf. Num. 21:1; Deut. 1:44). Libna, Adullam, and Makkedah were mentioned in 10:28-30. Bethel and Tappuah were in the hill country and Hepher, Laphek, and Lasharon were on the coastal plain. The first four of the eleven cities in the north were in the northern alliance (cf. 11:1). Taanach and Megiddo were key cities guarding a pass from the coast to the valley of Jezreel. The location of Kedesh is uncertain. Jokneam is at the foot of Mount Carmel. Dor was a well known city near the coast (cf. 11:2). The reference to the "people of Gilgal" is uncertain. Tirza is central, north of modern day Nablus.

In Conclusion

Portions of Scripture like these are sometimes viewed as tedious to read and void of much teaching content. However, it was a good thing for Joshua to take stock of the victories won and to list the kings and cities he had defeated. Joshua had obeyed God's direction and had trusted God against enormous odds to gain these victories. We can be victorious in spiritual warfare when we reckon on Christ's victory over sin and live in the light of it by conquering—in Christ's strength—the sins that tend to dominate us. Like Joshua, we should take stock of spiritual victories and recognize that it is God who gives them. In this way it is healthy for believers to review God's work in our lives and to give Him the glory. This kind of review encourages us to persevere until we reach the eternal rest promised to us.

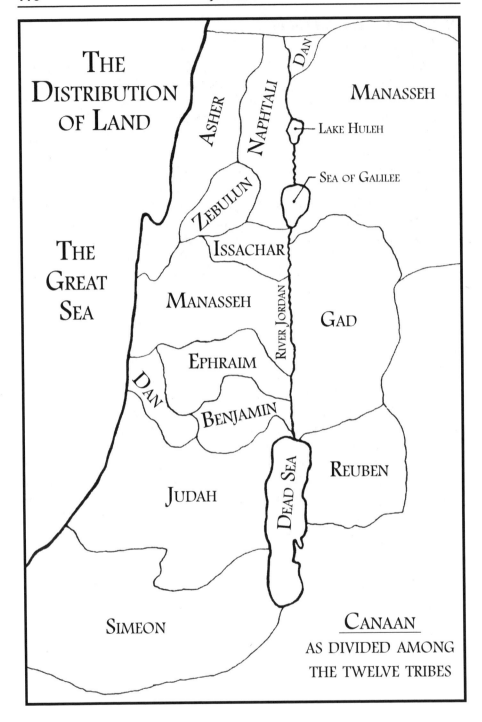

Joshua 13

Division of the Land East of Jordan

The conquest of the land had been accomplished. The next step was to apportion it among the twelve tribes of Israel. The stories of battles are replaced by descriptions of land areas and long lists of boundaries and cities as they are assigned to the various tribes. There are several reasons why these chapters are important and should not be skimmed over, despite their seeming irrelevance.

- They testify to the fulfillment of a promise. God had promised each tribe its own inheritance in the land that He was giving to Israel. Each tribe would praise Him in turn when His promise to them of their own borders was fulfilled. They could identify with what David the psalmist would write hundreds of years later: "The lines have fallen to me in pleasant places; Yes, I have a good inheritance" (Ps. 16:6).
- They record the borders of the land allotted to each tribe for which they were now responsible and accountable. Every one still had pockets of resistance to be defeated and areas of land to be possessed.
- In light of the fact that some of the land was still controlled by their enemies, these chapters lay the foundation for the story of Israel's struggles and wars that were to take place in the times of the judges and on into the times of the kings.
- The record of the borders is also for today, because not all the promised territory has even yet been fully occupied. In the coming Day of the Lord the land *will* be fully occupied. In that day the Jews will be gathered from the four corners of the earth and they will possess Edom, Moab, and Ammon from the tongue of the Sea of Egypt to the River (Isa. 11:11-16). It is fascinating for today's reader, because the land promised to them includes parts of the modern countries of Egypt, Jordan, Syria, and Lebanon, all of which are opposed to the existence of the modern state of Israel.

The Flow of Joshua 13 to 24

The material of Joshua 13 to 24 is arranged in logical order to explain how Joshua gave the land "as an inheritance to Israel" (11:23).

- Chapter 13:1-7 is the general introduction.
- Chapter 13:8-33 covers the distribution of land to the 2½ tribes on the east side of the Jordan.
- Chapters 14 through 19 record the division of land to the tribes on the west side of Jordan.
- Chapters 20 through 22 describe the cities of refuge and the altar of witness between the western and eastern tribes.
- Chapters 23 and 24 give the account of Joshua's farewell address and the renewal of the covenant at Shechem.

In the first half of the book it is God, not Joshua or the Israelites, who is clearly portrayed as the Warrior and Victor. In the second half of the book the prime Mover is still God. He is shown to be the Owner of the land and the Giver of it to His people. In these chapters He apportions the land as He sees fit and tells Joshua to divide it "as I have commanded you" (v. 6).

Joshua is Old (v. 1)

Joshua was an old man by the time the conquest was completed. Just how old is not entirely certain. At the time of the exodus he was of sufficient age to be chosen as the leader of Israel's army in fighting against the Amalekites (Ex. 17:8-10). When he and Caleb were chosen as two of the tribal representatives to spy out the land of Canaan, Caleb was forty-years-old (14:7). Since then forty-five more years had passed, and Caleb was now eighty-five (14:10). We conclude that Joshua was probably at least that old.

As Israel's God-given leader, it was extremely important for the division of the land to be accomplished before Joshua died. Without him the likelihood of strife over which tribe received which region would be much greater. The Lord then spoke to Joshua, as He had done many times before. This time He drew attention to his advanced age and the fact that there yet remained much land to be possessed (v. 1). Note that this phrase seems to contrast the statement in 11:23 that "Joshua took the whole land." What Joshua had done was to lead Israel in the major battles and in taking *general* control of all the land. There remained many unsecured areas and pockets of resistance. The task of each tribe would be to root out the resistant peoples within their allotted area. Thus, Joshua's immediate task was to apportion the land to the twelve tribes so that each tribe would then know the exact borders of the land for which they were responsible and in which they were to reap the rewards of the conquest.

The Land Remaining to be Possessed (vv. 2-6)

Before the actual apportionment was carried out, the Lord specified three areas as yet unconquered: some Philistine territory in the south (vv. 2-3), some additional Canaanite lands in the northern coastal area (v. 4), and some other territories in the mountainous areas to the north (vv. 5-6).

The Land of the Philistines

The Philistine people appear to have been part of a group known as the "sea peoples" who had migrated from the island of Crete, sometimes called Caphtor. They are mentioned in the table of nations (Gen. 10:14), and some of them were already in Gerar in the days of Abraham (Gen. 20:1). In Moses' day they were linked with the Caphtorim (Deut. 2:23), having settled along the coast from the Gaza region northward. Joshua had not encountered them in the invasion, but their land was part of Israel's inheritance. The Geshurites were also from the southwest and are referred to in David's day (1 Sam. 27:8).

The Philistines had invaded Canaanite territory; thus the whole Philistine area was to be taken over as part of their inheritance (Gen. 12:7; Ex. 3:8-9). The extent of the Philistine territory stretched from "Sihor, which is east of Egypt, as far as the border of Ekron northward" (v. 3). Sihor is probably a reference to the "brook of Egypt" (15:4, 47), a wadi, or dry valley, on its eastern border (cf. Jer. 2:18). It is called Wadi el Arish today. It forms the southwest border of Israel's inheritance, just as the Euphrates River does the northeastern border. Ekron, the most northern city of the five major Philistine cities, is also called Timnah in the book of Judges (Judg. 14:1). None of the Philistines cities of Gaza, Ashdod, Ashkelon, Gath or Ekron were destroyed by the Israelites. They remained as a thorn in Israel's side for centuries. Also mentioned here are the Avites, who seem to have been the original Canaanite peoples of the southern coastal area (v. 3; Deut. 2:23).

The Land of the Canaanites

The second area mentioned is the coastal area immediately north of the Philistine area in what is known today as southwestern Lebanon (vv. 2-3). The site of Mearah is not known except that it belonged to the Sidonians. The Aphek mentioned here is not the city of the central coastal plain but a northern site, perhaps the town of Afqa, north of Beirut. Another extremity of the land to be conquered was the territory of the Amorites.

The Land of Lebanon

The third area that was still unconquered is the Lebanon of today. The Gebalites were from Gebal, better known as Biblos, north of Beirut. Extensive ruins still exist there today. "Baal Gad below Mount Hermon" marks the southern end of the Bekah Valley, and "the entrance to Hamath," the northern end. It is mentioned elsewhere as a boundary city (Num. 13:21, 1 Kings 8:65). Also included was the mountainous region of Lebanon as far as the Brook Misrephoth and all the Sidonians (v. 6).

These God-given (yet unconquered) territories were both a constant source of irritation and a challenge to obedience for the Israelites throughout their history. Their continuing conflict with the enemy parallels our Christian experience, for our lives here on earth are marked by ongoing spiritual conflict in which we must engage if we are to bring different areas of threat under control.

"Them I will drive out"

God then told Joshua that He, God, would be responsible to drive these yet unconquered peoples from before the children of Israel. It would be Joshua's responsibility to divide the land among the tribes. When Joshua fulfilled his responsibility (v. 6) God would dispossess Israel's enemies. It is a good lesson for us that we are to be concerned only with the job that God has given us to do and not to seek to do things that God would do in some other way.

A Review of Apportioning the Land East of Jordan (vv. 7-13)

Joshua now reviews the boundaries of the land on the east side of Jordan which had been captured and distributed by Moses. Rather than specifically delineating the land given to each of the 2½ tribes, he describes the whole area and mentions some of the parts still to be captured. In doing this Joshua emphasized the unity of the nation on both sides of the Jordan. Just as Moses had distributed the land to the 2½ tribes on the east side, so Joshua would distribute the land to the 9½ tribes on the west side.

Joshua describes the territory east of the Jordan generally from the south to the north, starting from Aroer on the banks of the River Arnon, the southernmost point of Israel's territory on the east side, close to the northern border of Moab. From there he moves north to Medeba and also mentioned Dibon, an important city between them. Then he lists all the cities Moses had taken that were ruled by King Sihon from his capital in Heshbon. These people were Amorites. North of them were the Ammonites and Gileadites. Farther north toward Mount Hermon and Bashan was where the Geshurites and the Maachathites lived. Og had been king of Bashan before being defeated. The reminder of Og's defeat on the east side would be an encouragement to those who still faced giants on the west side.

The next statement begins with "Nevertheless," regarding the Geshurites and Maachathites who were defeated by Moses but not driven out (v. 13; 12:5). The fact that they tolerated their continued presence sets an ominous pattern for the rest of Joshua (cf. 10:40-43) and later. In the time of David, the Geshurite princess whom David married was the wife who bore him Absalom (2 Sam. 3:3). When Absalom murdered Amnon he took refuge in Geshur (2 Sam. 13:38). Still later the Maachathites joined in the Ammonite rebellion against David (2 Sam. 10:6-8). It was in that war that Uriah, Bathsheba's husband, was killed. It is interesting that the two great failures of David's life—his liaison with Bathsheba and Absalom's rebellion—were associated with the Maachathites and the Geshurites. These consequences of Israel's incomplete obedience ought to be a powerful deterrent to us when we are similarly tempted to be satisfied with only partial victory.

The Inheritance of Levi (v. 14)

After summarizing the boundaries of the lands already captured and those still to be taken on the east side, Joshua explains the inheritance of the tribe of Levi: "Only to the tribe of Levi He had given no inheritance; the sacrifices of the LORD God of Israel made by fire are their inheritance." A strong emphasis is placed on the first word "only," indicating that their inheritance was entirely different from that of the other tribes (v. 14; cf. v. 33; 14:3). This confirms what Moses had said in Deuteronomy 18:1. Moses had gone on to say, "I have given the children of Levi all the tithes in Israel as an inheritance in return for the work which they perform" (Num. 18:21-24). The Levites would not only receive the monetary tithes but would be given the best parts of the animal sacrifices brought by the people, together with their offerings of first fruits consisting of grain, wine, oil, and fleece (Deut. 10:8-9).

The offerings and sacrifices were to be compensation to the Levites for their priestly service because the Lord had chosen them to minister in His name (Deut.18:2-5). Their ministry was vital to the spiritual health of God's people. The Levites, in return, were to be generously supported in their ministry. We can draw from this a biblical principle that the material support of those who give themselves to God's service should come from those who benefit spiritually from that service. Paul speaks of reaping "material things" from the Corinthian church because he had sown "spiritual things" for them (1 Cor. 9:11). He also spoke of church elders who labor "in the word and doctrine" being worthy to receive wages (1 Tim. 5:17-18).

Another reason for the Levites' separate inheritance is a consequence of their history. Jacob's son Levi (along with Simeon) had committed terrible atrocities at Shechem (Gen. 34:25-31). As a result, the tribe was to be scattered in Israel (Gen. 49:5-7). Later, however, following the incident of worshiping the golden calf, the tribe of Levi alone chose to stand "on the Lord's side" with Moses. They obeyed Moses' command to execute the offenders (Ex. 32:26-28). Near the end of their wilderness journey the Levite Phinehas, grandson of Aaron, stood against the idolatry and immorality of the Israelites, so his descendants were promised an "everlasting priesthood" (Num. 25:1-13). In Moses' final address he remembered the Levites' faithfulness to God when the other Israelites were complaining at Meribah (Num. 20:2-13), and he promised that the Levites would be teachers of the law and leaders in worship for all of Israel (Deut. 33:8-11). Their history may be an encouragement to those who forfeit their place in God's service due to sin: in God's grace, it is possible to recover and be restored to some effective ministry for Him among His people.

The Inheritance of Reuben (vv. 15-23)

The remainder of the chapter is given over to the review of the allotments made by Moses to the 2½ tribes on the east side of Jordan, beginning with

Reuben, the tribe of Jacob's firstborn son. The often used phrase in this passage "according to their families" means that each family was given a specific place (v. 18; cf. vv. 24, 29; 15:1, 12, etc.). Reuben's inheritance is carefully described by naming a number of cities that were contained in it. The area was bounded on the south by the Arnon River, on the east by the desert, on the north by a line from Mephaath, on the east by Beth Jeshimoth, and on the west by the mouth of the Jordan and the Dead Sea. Two of the cities mentioned became Levitical cities (Jahaza and Kedemoth) which were given to the Levites to live in (v. 18).

Bamoth-baal (literally, "Heights of Baal") is where the prophet ("soothsayer") Balaam had tried to curse Israel (v. 17; Num. 22:41). The mention of Balaam's death may have been a warning to the Reubenites in case they sought to repeat the apostasy that Balaam had instigated. The account of it is repeated a number of times in Scripture (24:9; Deut. 23:4-5, Neh. 13:2; Mic. 6:5). The description of Reuben's inheritance closes with a mention of the border at the Jordan River (v. 23). The word "villages" refers to the un-walled communities surrounding a walled city, the whole of which was a city-state.

The Inheritance of Gad (vv. 24-28)

Gad's territory was in-between the territories of Reuben to the south and the half of Manasseh to the north. Its western boundary was the entire length of the Jordan River from the Sea of Galilee to the Dead Sea. It was bounded on the east by the frontiers of the part of Ammonite territory left untouched by Moses. The whole territory of Gad was the southern part of a far larger area known as Gilead. Rabbah was the capital of the Ammonites and is the same as modern Amman, Jordan.

The Inheritance of Eastern Manasseh (vv. 29-31)

The territory given to the half tribe of Manasseh extended northward from Gad's territory as far as Mount Hermon. Its western boundary was from the Sea of Galilee north along the upper Jordan. It included the northern part of the region of Gilead and all of Bashan where King Og had ruled. Bashan was especially valuable because the high plateau was surrounded by forested mountains and made for rich pastureland for cattle (Jer. 50:19; Ezek. 39:18; Mic. 7:14). Machir, who is specially mentioned, was a son of Manasseh and grandson of Joseph. His descendants had captured this region from Og (Num. 32:39-40; Deut. 3:15).

Levi's Inheritance: the Lord Himself (v. 33)

The final verse of chapter 13 adds one more element to the inheritance that the priestly tribe of Levi received. In verse 14 their inheritance was to be the sacrifices brought by the worshipping Israelites. Here it is defined as the Lord Himself: "The LORD God of Israel was their inheritance" (v. 33). Aaron, the Levite and high priest during the wilderness wanderings, was clearly told by the

Lord, "You shall have no inheritance in their land . . . I am your portion and your inheritance" (Num. 18:20-21). The Lord was closely identified with the sacrifices. The Levites, because they were dealing with offerings to the Lord continually, would gain a greater knowledge and appreciation of God than the ordinary Israelites. In this way the Lord would be their portion. In a similar way, believers today grow in their personal knowledge of God and His attributes as they engage in praying to Him, worshiping Him, studying His Word, and serving Him.

In Conclusion

Let us remember three lessons from this chapter. First, for God's people there is always more "land" to be possessed (v. 1). That is, God desires to give us portions of our spiritual blessings in Christ that we have not fully taken to be our own. Satan, the world, and our flesh want to keep us from enjoying them, so we must diligently fight for them. Second, God provides materially for those who give themselves to spiritual service through the offerings of His people (v. 14). The best lesson of all is that those who are most fully engaged in spiritual worship and service will best obtain the inheritance of knowing God Himself, of sensing His nearness, and of finding delight in His grace to the highest degree.

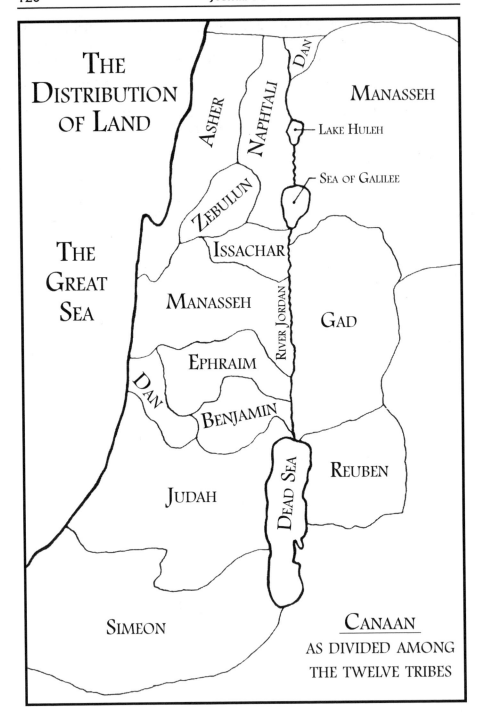

How / WHAT IS SANTIFICATION? Romans 12, 1+2

1 Cor 6:9
Epher 1 chpt 4 chpt
1 Thess 5
2 Tim 2
Heb 13

Rom chpt 5 –

What to do when sin is in Camp?
- Run to GOD
- Don't blame GOD for your sin
-

5 - Don't lay in self-pity
6 - Repent (turn back)

8 - when you sin, confess

(Chpt 6 - Romans)

Chpt 8
Restored fellowship with GOD will bring Victory

SET APART FOR THE SERVICE OF GOD.

1 COR 6:11
- Chpt 13
- " :14
- Start Chpt 15

Rom 12:3-8 — gifts to all believers → 1 COR 12:4-27

QUES: WHAT KIND OF DEATH DID CHRIST DIE — LUKE 23, GAL:3, PHIL:2

LUKE 23:44   GAL:3:-13   PHIL 2:8

Rom 6:12-14

Eph 6:12

Chpt 17

WHO WILL BE SAVED?
- Isa 55:3-7
- Luke 13:3,5
- " 24:47
- John 3:5
- " 6:47
- Rev 18 + 19

Start 20

WHAT DOES IT MEAN TO REPENT
- II Chron 7:14v
- II Corn 7:8-10

Chpt 21, 22

JOSHUA 14

The Inheritances of Caleb and the Tribe of Judah

Beginning with chapter 14, Joshua explains how he distributed the land to the 9½ tribes on the west side of the Jordan. This distribution takes up the next seven chapters, beginning with Judah, the leading tribe (14-16). He then describes the allotments to the tribes that were named after Joseph's sons, Ephraim and Manasseh (16-17). Finally he summarizes the allotment of the remaining seven tribes (18-19). The allotments appear to have been made in two different places. The tribal allotments to Judah and Joseph were made at Gilgal (14:6; cf. 4:19; 5:9), while the allotments to the other seven tribes were made from Shiloh where the tabernacle was set up (18:1).

Dividing the Land by Lot (vv. 1-5)

The actual division of the land was administered by Eleazar the priest (Aaron's son and successor), Joshua, and "the heads of the fathers of the tribes" (v. 1). Eleazar is mentioned first, in relation to the spiritual dimension of dividing the land. The Lord was to be central in the entire process. Joshua was involved because, as their leader and military commander, he could ensure that the process was smooth and orderly. Finally, the "heads of the fathers of the tribes" were included in the process as those directly responsible for the welfare of their people. Thus, the spiritual leader, the political leader, and the tribal heads were all involved in the distribution.

Lots were used to determine the specific inheritance of each tribe, as God had commanded through Moses (v. 2; Num. 26:52-56; 33:54; 34:13). In using lots they were not depending on chance but deliberately trusting that God would cause the lot of each tribe to line up with His predetermined will. As such, casting lots was a means of determining God's guidance outside the bounds of human choice: "Its every decision is from the LORD" (Prov. 16:33). The precise method of casting lots in biblical times is not described anywhere in Scripture.

Once again Joshua informs us that the tribe of Levi would not receive a land inheritance. He also states that the tribe of Joseph would receive two allotments named after his sons Ephraim and Manasseh (vv. 3-4; cf. 13:33).

The Levites did, however, receive certain cities within the other tribal allotments that are named in chapter 21. In this way the total of twelve tribes is retained in the nation of Israel, a number consistently used all through Scripture (Rev. 21:12). The importance of these introductory verses is that, in dividing the land, the Israelites were obeying the Lord: "As the LORD commanded . . . so the children of Israel did" (v. 5; cf. 1:17; 11:15; 22:9; 24:14).

The Inheritance of Caleb (vv. 6-15)

Caleb was among the representatives of the tribe of Judah who came to Joshua in Gilgal to settle the matter of Judah's inheritance. Caleb is called the Son of Jephunneh, the Kenizzite. Caleb reminded Joshua of what the Lord said to Moses concerning them. They were the only two of the twelve spies at Kadesh Barnea who had believed that God would give His people the land that flowed with milk and honey (Num. 14:6-9). He had personally brought back word to Moses "as it was in my heart" (v. 7), but the ten spies did not believe that God would give them the land. The majority's conviction was so convincing that they "made the heart of the people melt." In contrast to their unbelief, Caleb's testimony was that he "wholly followed" the Lord (v. 8).

Caleb's Request

Caleb went on to remind Joshua that Moses had made an oath that Caleb should receive a personal inheritance (v. 9; cf. v. 6). Because Caleb believed that the children of Israel were well able to take the area occupied by giants (Num. 13:30), God said to Moses, "My servant Caleb, because he has a different spirit in him, and has followed Me fully, I will bring into the land where he went, and his descendants shall inherit it" (Num. 14:24). Caleb took this promise to Moses as if it were an oath, even though neither the word "swear" nor "oath" appears in the text. Caleb reasoned that God had kept him alive for forty-five years until "this day" in order to fulfill His promise.

Caleb then switched from the past to the present, using the phrase "and now" twice in verse 10. He mentioned his age: eighty-five. Neither the long arduous trip through the wilderness nor the battles fought in Canaan had dampened his spirit. He informed Joshua that he was as strong at that moment as he had been when he was sent out to spy on Canaan (v. 11). He also said that his strength for war, "for going out and for coming in," was as vigorous as ever.

"Give me this mountain" (v. 12)

Based on all he had just said, Caleb boldly asked for "this mountain" as his own inheritance. He was referring to the hill country around the city of Hebron, although he did not mention it by name (cf. v. 14). He knew the Anakim were there and that their cities were large and well fortified. The giants had struck fear into the hearts of the Israelites many years before, but Caleb's faith was as strong as ever, and he proclaimed to Joshua, "It may be that the LORD will be with me and that I shall be able to drive them out as the LORD said." When he said "it may be," he was not expressing doubt but rather his strong conviction that God would be true to His word. The story of the battle for Hebron and the defeat of the Anakim is told in 11:21-22. In this present passage we learn of the part that Caleb played in it. His faith in God's promise was the key to his conquest.

Caleb's Inheritance (vv. 13-15)

Joshua's response to Caleb's impassioned plea was to bless him and to grant him Hebron as his inheritance. It was not just a personal favor to his friend, because we read in 15:13 that Joshua blessed him and granted Caleb this inheritance "according to the commandment of the LORD." When he "blessed" Caleb, Joshua was granting God's favor upon him in the upcoming battle to capture Hebron (v. 13). The blessing would encompass the quality of his future life there, the prosperity of enjoying God, the growth of his family, and the increase of material possessions.

Caleb is again identified by his full name, "the son of Jephunneh the Kenizzite." It is possible that the use of his full name emphasizes the pagan ancestry (Gen. 15:19) from which he had been converted. Since then he had wholly followed the Lord—as one of the twelve spies, as a leader during the wilderness wanderings, and as a soldier in the invasion of Canaan. As a result, God rewarded him with both an inheritance and a blessing. The evidence of the blessing was that, "to this day" (the day of writing the book of Joshua) Caleb's family lived in Hebron (v. 14).

Caleb's Example to Us

Caleb is an outstanding example of how God rewards faith and faithfulness. He did not just *wait* for forty-five years; he exercised godly patience and wholly followed the Lord during that time. God kept His promise and Caleb received his inheritance. We too must persevere in patience, as Caleb did. We can trust God to be faithful to us, as He was to Caleb.

Chapter 14 ends with a comment on the name of the city of Hebron and its former name of Kirjath Arba (cf. Gen. 23:2). Arba was called the "greatest man among the Anakim" in this passage, which can be taken to mean that he was the tallest of the giants.

In Conclusion

The final phrase is, "Then the land had rest from war" (v. 15). The *rest* of victory is a continuing theme in Joshua beginning with Moses' promise to Joshua that the Lord would give Israel rest (1:13-15). It comes into focus again at the conclusion of the summary of Joshua's victories (11:23). Now it concludes the Caleb story of victory at Hebron. It is a fitting conclusion, because Caleb's faith in God and his courage to conquer were an inspiration to the Israelites to fully conquer the land and gain *rest* by removing the Canaanites (13:1). It is a prime example of God's intention for the conquest of Canaan. Caleb claimed by faith what God had promised, and he fought with courage to obtain it.

Joshua 15

The Boundaries and Cities of Judah's Inheritance

Hundreds of years before the conquest of Canaan, Jacob's dying blessing had indicated that Judah, although his fourth-born son, was to have the authority, "the scepter," over the other tribes (Gen. 49:8-12). The dynasty of King David would arise from Judah, and ultimately Messiah would emerge from that tribe. It is no surprise, therefore, that Joshua describes Judah's inheritance first. It is not only given first, it is also the most detailed and the longest. Joshua 15 summarizes two elements in Judah's inheritance: the boundaries of the land they would occupy and a list of the cities within the boundaries described.

As with all passages of this nature given in the Scriptures, the reader will gain the most understanding if he or she locates these places on a map while reading the text.

The Boundaries of Judah (vv. 1-12)

The borders of Judah are described in the same way as an estate owner would describe the boundaries to a friend who was going to walk around them. Many different verbs are used, leaving a strong visual impression: "began . . . went out . . . passed along . . . went around . . . went up . . . went down . . . turned . . . continued . . . went up to the top . . . ended." Not all the place names mentioned are known to modern scholars, but enough are known to give a clear idea of the ancient boundary. Joshua starts in the southeast corner of Judah's allotment, from a point where the southern end of the Dead Sea met the northern border of Edom (vv. 1-2). From there the border went southwest through the Wilderness of Zin, passing Kadesh Barnea and on to the Brook of Egypt. From there it went northwest along the Wadi to meet the Mediterranean Sea. "This shall be your southern border" (vv. 1-4).

Caleb's Victories at Hebron and Debir (vv. 13-20)

Joshua includes here a second reference about Caleb's special inheritance at Hebron (cf. 14:6-15). Although similar to the chapter 14 passage, some details are added. We learn that it was the Lord who commanded Joshua to grant the inheritance to Caleb (v. 13). In the Bible record the Lord first gave this command to Moses (Num. 14:24). Joshua took the commands given by Moses as commands from the Lord.

We also learn from this passage that Caleb drove out three giants from Hebron in the battle. Many years earlier, Caleb had noted these same three giants by name when he had spied out the land (Num. 13:22). Their fame was widely known (Deut. 9:2). It seems like poetic justice that God used Caleb to drive them out!

The Conquest of Debir

Debir was a city near Hebron. Its capture is recorded earlier, as part of Joshua's southern campaign (10:36-39). Some commentators believe that the city was first captured by Joshua, then retaken by Canaanites, and captured again as recorded in this passage. It is more likely that what we have recorded here is additional detail as to how it was captured during the southern campaign. Debir's ancient name was Kirjath Sepher, which means "city of books," or "city of scribes." It may have had a library for Canaanite records.

Caleb offered his daughter Achsah in marriage to any brave man who would capture the city. Other instances of this practice may be found in Scripture (cf. 1 Sam. 17:25). Othniel the son of Kenaz, Caleb's younger brother, accepted the challenge and took the city (Judg. 1:13). Later, when Achsah arrived, she "persuaded" (the Hebrew word is a strong term meaning "to incite") Othniel to ask her father Caleb for a field in addition to the city of Debir. We hear nothing more of Othniel in this passage, although we may assume that he did ask and that the "field" was granted. But apparently Achsah yearned for more. When she later visited her father she requested a "blessing" or marriage gift, saying, "Since you have given me land in the South, give me also springs of water" (v. 19). Having been blessed by God himself, Caleb generously blessed his daughter by giving her both the "upper springs" and the "lower springs"—a reminder that we should freely share what God has blessed us with.

The description about the boundaries of the tribe of Judah's inheritance and the stories of Caleb and Othniel conclude with the statement, "This was the inheritance of the tribe of the children of Judah according to their families" (v. 20). The pattern of describing the boundaries, followed by a summary statement and a listing the cities within those boundaries, forms a pattern for this section of Joshua.

The Cities of Judah's Inheritance (vv. 21-63)

Beginning with a short summary statement, a long list of the names of cities that Judah inherited is provided. The purpose of the list was to remind the Israelites that God had kept His promise to them literally in giving them the land with all its cities. One hundred-and-twenty-two cities are listed, half of which are mentioned nowhere else in the Bible. A list like this places the people of the Bible in time and space for us. It helps us to better understand the setting in which God worked out His plan of redemption. We should notice that Judah's many cities indicate Judah's importance among the tribes of Israel. The list of its cities can be divided into the four geographical sections of Judah itself: those in the *southland* (the Negev, vv. 21-32), those in the *western foothills* (the Shepelah, vv. 33-47), those in the *hill country* (vv. 48-60), and those in the *desert* (vv. 61-62).

A careful reader may notice that the running totals of the cities given are not always the same as the actual number of cities listed. For example: thirty-six southland cities are listed in verses 21-32, but the total given in verse 32 is twenty-nine. A possible reason for this may be that some of the cities were too small to be listed in the running total. Also, some cities have the same name as others (such as Hazor), and additional study may be required to distinguish them. Other technical questions will present themselves to students but are outside the scope of this commentary.

The list ends with one significant failure of Judah in their quest to drive out the inhabitants of one of their cities. The city was Jerusalem, on the border between Judah and Benjamin. Joshua was said to have defeated the king of Jerusalem, but evidently he did not capture the city (12:7-10). An almost identical verse in Judges 1:21 blames Benjamin for failing to drive out the Jebusites. This may be because the boundary appears to put the city in Benjamin's territory (vv. 7-8) or because Jerusalem was not strongly identified with either tribe. Eventually King David from the tribe of Judah captured it from the Jebusites four hundred years later (2 Sam. 5:5-10). In the meantime Judah and Benjamin's inability to take Jerusalem demonstrated a failure of faith in God. There is no record that they even tried. The people of Judah dwelling with the pagan Jebusites resulted in a situation of compromise.

In Conclusion

There is a lesson in this chapter for believers who allow strongholds of sin to coexist with their faith in God. In such situations one's faith is always weakened. What a contrast to the great faith of Caleb, who believed God would give him Hebron, the city known for its giants. He acted on his belief and God delivered the city into his hands. Othniel saw Caleb's faith and followed it by taking Debir and claiming Achsah, Caleb's daughter, as his wife. She too had both the faith and the boldness to ask for springs of water, which were granted to her. Caleb's faith strengthened the faith of both Othniel and of Achsah. Our faith, too, put into practice, will strengthen other believers.

Joshua 16

The Inheritance of Joseph

The inheritance of the tribe of Joseph follows that of Judah. Joseph was Jacob's favored son. When Jacob came to join Joseph in Egypt, he adopted Joseph's two sons, Ephraim and Manasseh, so that they would each receive a full share of the inheritance (Gen. 48:5). When Jacob blessed his sons, Joseph, like Judah, received a more extensive and detailed blessing than their brothers (Gen. 49:8-12, 22-26). When the children of Israel came into the land, Joseph was awarded a double inheritance to accommodate both Ephraim and Manasseh. Of these two tribes, Ephraim received the larger allotment, just as Jacob had indicated when he crossed his hands in blessing them so that Ephraim, the younger, received priority over Manasseh the firstborn (Gen. 48:15-20).

When Joshua drew the lot for Joseph, he was still in Gilgal (14:6; 15:1). The allotment for half of the tribe of Manasseh had previously been made by Moses on the east of Jordan (13:29-33). Here Joshua draws another lot for the remainder of the tribe of Joseph on the west side of the Jordan, which was to be divided between the entire tribe of Ephraim and the other half of tribe of Manasseh. The first four verses of chapter 16 describe the whole territory given to the two tribes of Joseph. Verses 5 to 10 focus on the allotment for Ephraim, and chapter 17 focuses on the allotment given to Manasseh.

The Boundary of Ephraim and Manasseh (vv. 1-4)

The east/west line described here marks only the southern border of Joseph's inheritance. Just one lot was drawn for the "children of Joseph"; the word is in the singular. It indicates that the author wants us to understand that the whole house of Joseph was considered one unit (cf. v. 4; 17:14). Almost the entire boundary described is that of Ephraim, but it is viewed here as the boundary of the whole tribe of Joseph, another indication that they are seen as one. The description of this line began near Jericho in the Jordan valley and ran westward through the dry hills up from the Jordan Valley to Bethel and Luz in the hill country. It continued past the land of the Arkites and an unknown place called Attaroth and then past lower Beth Horon to the large Canaanite city of Gezer and on to the sea. South of this line and between the territory of Ephraim and the territory of Judah was a narrow corridor, the inheritance of Benjamin and

Dan. This line between Ephraim and Benjamin would become important in later history in that it would mark the dividing line between the kingdoms of Judah and Israel.

Bethel and Luz are distinguished here, though several times in the Bible they are regarded as synonymous (18:13; Gen. 28:19; Judges 1:23). Some have suggested that the name Bethel was given to the spot where Jacob had seen his vision near the city of Luz and that it later became so important that the city of Luz was called Bethel. The Arkites were apparently a known Canaanite people. David's trusted counselor Hushai was an Arkite (2 Sam. 5:32). The boundary ended at the Mediterranean Sea, probably northwest of Gezer. The coastal area was Philistine territory and, thus, only theoretically part of Ephraim, because they never drove the Philistines out.

The Boundaries of Ephraim (vv. 5-10)

Joshua now focuses on the territory of the tribe of Ephraim, which was in the very center of the country. He begins with an abbreviated summary of the southern border that was previously described as the southern border of the combined border of Ephraim and Manasseh (v. 5). He then describes the northern border; beginning at a central point called Michmethath, (near Shechem). From there it went southeast to Jericho and the Jordan, where it connected with the southern boundary (vv. 6-7). Westward from Michmethath it went along the valley of the brook Kanah (modern Wadi Qanah) all the way to the sea where it connected with the southern boundary (v. 8a). Some of Ephraim's cities were located in the territory of Manasseh, although the reason for this is not given (v. 9). It has been suggested that perhaps Jacob's greater blessing on Ephraim might explain it.

The description of Ephraim's territory closes with a note about their failure to drive out the Canaanites who dwelt in Gezer (v. 10; Judg. 1:29). Earlier, Joshua had defeated the king of Gezer when he had come with his army to help the city of Lachish fight against Joshua. Joshua won that battle "until he left him none remaining" (10:33; 12:12), but evidently he had not moved on to capture the city. Gezer was an important city of the Canaanites being strategically built on the road from Jerusalem to Joppa not far from the main road connecting Egypt to Mesopotamia. After the conquest of Canaan it remained an independent city until the days of Solomon when the Egyptian Pharaoh took it and gave it to his daughter as a wedding gift on her marriage to Solomon (1 Kings 9:15-17).

While the Ephraimites failed to capture and destroy Gezer, they did compel the people of Gezer to become "forced laborers" (v. 10). God, however, had commanded them to completely destroy all the people (Deut. 20:16-18). Thus they failed to keep God's commandment. God permitted the Israelites to put those people who lived far away from Canaan under tribute, as they did with the deceitful Gibeonites, for Joshua *thought* they lived far away (9:27). In the case of the Ephraimites though, it was incomplete obedience to offer a compromise to the people of Gezer.

In Conclusion

Once again, Israel's experience serves to warn us about an aspect of the spiritual warfare we wage. We must beware of settling for compromise. Instead of allowing sin a place in our lives, seemingly under control, we should drive it out using the power that the indwelling Holy Spirit makes available to us.

Joshua 17

Issues Relating to Manasseh and Ephraim

With Ephraim's allotment settled, Joshua turns our attention to Manasseh's territory in chapter 17. He begins by providing some background information that will help clarify some statements in the chapter.

Manasseh, Machir, and Gilead (v. 1)

First he reminds us that Manasseh was Joseph's firstborn son. This gives us perspective on all the genealogical information about him. Manasseh had only one son, Machir, here called his firstborn because inheritance rights are in view (v. 1; Num. 26:29). Machir was the "father of Gilead," a name which has two connections with Manasseh's inheritance. The first relates to the land of Gilead on the east side of the Jordan which had been captured by Manasseh's "men of war" (v. 1). The land was called the land of Gilead and Bashan (Num. 32:39). The other connection with the name "father of Gilead" is that Machir had a son named Gilead who had six sons. Their names are given in verse 2 (cf. Num. 26:30-32). Thus, Gilead was not only the name of the land they inherited on the east side, but the name of an ancestor of the tribe of Manasseh.

Zelophehad's Family (vv. 2-3)

One of the sons of Gilead, Hepher, had a son named Zelophehad (vv. 2-3). All the names in the line of Manasseh may seem irrelevant to the reader but they are necessary to the point of the story about who gets a share of the inheritance on the west side of Jordan. Zelophehad was the great-great grandson of Manasseh who had joined with the half of his tribe to fight with Joshua on the west side for a share of the land, along with other family members. The problem was that Zelophehad had five daughters, and since the inheritance was usually only passed down to sons, Zelophehad's family was in danger of losing their inheritance. Before Joshua took leadership, these five daughters approached Moses to explain their situation (Num. 27:1-11). Moses appealed to the Lord, who told him that the five daughters could indeed receive their father's inheritance. Moses extended it beyond Zelophehad's daughters to make it a law that the inheritance of any man who died without sons would go to his daughters.

The Request of Zelophehad's Daughters (vv. 3-6)

Now that Joshua was overseeing allotments to the twelve tribes, Zelophehad's five daughters took the opportunity to remind Eleazer, Joshua, and the tribal leaders of God's approval of them receiving their father's allotment. They were now claiming it officially. Joshua responded readily that they should receive an inheritance "among their father's brothers" to fulfill God's will (v. 4).

The daughters received more than they asked for: not just one portion, but one portion each like the brothers of their grandfather Hepher. There were ten tracts of land on the west bank of the Jordan given to the tribe of Manasseh. Five of these went to five of Gilead's six sons. The remaining five tracts went to the descendants of Gilead's sixth son Hepher, the daughters of his son Zelophehad. This whole incident shows that the place women had in God's eyes and in Jewish society was not nearly as limited as is often claimed. It also shows the value placed by both God and His people on the continuing possession of the land. As believers in Christ we should place the highest value on the inheritance God has provided to us in Him.

The Boundaries of Manasseh's Inheritance (vv. 7-11)

The borders of Manasseh's territory explained here are not nearly as precise as those of Judah and Ephraim. The description begins with a northern point where Manasseh's territory joined the border of Asher and a southern point where it met the border of Ephraim near Shechem (16:6). Generally, Manasseh's territory was north of Ephraim, east of the Mediterranean Sea, west of the Jordan (not mentioned here), and south of the territories of Asher and Issachar (vv. 7-10). It included some forested hill country and most of the valley of Jezreel, the richest agricultural area in Israel. Six cities are mentioned in Manasseh's allotment, all in the valley of Jezreel, except for Dor which was on the coast (v. 11). Among them, Beth Shean and Megiddo were among the largest in Canaanite Israel. Both cities feature strongly in the biblical record. Their impressive ruins are a tourist attraction today.

The Failure of Manasseh (vv. 12-13)

Manasseh had failed to drive out all the Geshurites and the Maachathites on the east side of Jordan in previous years (13:13). The tribe of Judah had failed to drive the Jebusites out from Jerusalem (15:63). Ephraim failed to drive the Canaanites out of Gezer (16:10). Now it is recorded that the tribe of Manasseh was guilty of failing to drive out or destroy the inhabitants of these powerful cities in the valley of Jezreel (v. 12). Instead, when they defeated a town, they merely put the people into forced labor, a practice which violated God's instruction to utterly destroy the Canaanites (Deut. 20:16-18).

In tolerating the pagans and using them for their own advantage rather than destroying them, they were preparing the way for their own destruction in the future. Moses had strictly warned them of the danger of being tempted to worship the Canaanite gods (Deut. 12:29-30). The book of Judges sadly records that this very thing happened all too quickly (Judg. 2:11-12). Incomplete obedience and compromise eventually led the nation of Israel to slide into idolatry and ultimately into judgment. The application of this danger in the lives of Christians surrounded by worldliness and ungodliness is all to clear: "Love not the world."

The Complaint of the Tribe of Joseph (vv. 14-18)

The allotments of land made to Ephraim and Manasseh ends with a complaint. Together they had received only one "lot," but that lot was large, as any map of the tribal territories will show (16:1). Indeed, they had land on the east side of the Jordan as well as a large portion on the west side in the center of the land. Their complaint reflected that they were not satisfied with their allotment; they came to Joshua and asked, "Why have you given us but one lot and one portion to inherit?" (v. 14). To strengthen their complaint they declared they were "a great people inasmuch as the LORD has blessed us until now."

Their request can be compared to Caleb's request (14:6-12), as well as that of the daughters of Zelophehad (v. 4), but there is a significant difference in that those requests were both based on clear promises to them from the Lord. Manasseh and Ephraim were simply complaining that the allotment they had been given was not large enough. How could they continue to be blessed of God (to prosper and grow) without more land? Joshua's reply implied that they were arrogant. Their second complaint was that the people who lived in the Valley of Jezreel had iron chariots. They believed that they had no hope of defeating people who had superior armory to their own. Like the unbelieving ten spies in Numbers 13, these two tribes were neglecting to bring God into the equation. Though Joshua himself was an Ephraimite, he granted them no undue favors.

Joshua spoke to them with force, "You are a great people and have great power; you shall not have one lot only, but the mountain country shall be yours" (vv. 17-18), telling them that they should fully utilize the land they had. Their portion was given by lot; therefore it was God's choice for them. They boasted about how many people they had so Joshua said in effect, "Just go in and clear it of the trees right to the edges." Then, when had they finished clearing the wooded land, they could go into the plain and drive out the Canaanites. Thus they would have the Valley of Jezreel as well "though they have iron chariots and are strong." His rebuke is sarcastic because they were greedy for more when they had not utilized what they had been given.

In Conclusion

The example of Ephraim and Manasseh is a strong reminder to us as believers to not seek more from God when we have not fully made use of the gifts God has given us by His choice. We need to "clear the land" we already have of the "trees" that keep us from spiritual productivity and greater blessing. These "trees" are anything that gets in the way of obedience and faith. We need to face the enemies we have and see God give us victory in our lives. When the "trees" are gone, we can then move out into the place where the enemy is strong and armed with "chariots." There we have the promise of God that we can "drive out the Canaanites" and possess the rich land they presently occupy. It is usually true that the richest part of our inheritance has the most enemies to displace. Let us stop complaining about the lot God has given us and instead use what we have received to its fullest.

JOSHUA 18-19

The Distribution of Land at Shiloh

Chapters 18 and 19 belong together. They deal with the inheritances of the remaining seven tribes. All seven are treated in the same way, and all the descriptions of their inherited lands are shorter than those of the more important tribes of Judah and Joseph in chapters 15-17. This distribution was made at Shiloh rather than at Gilgal. This time the whole of the remaining land was surveyed and divided into seven portions. Then they cast lots to determine which portion each of them would receive. These chapters also repeat some information already given about the inheritance of the 2½ tribes east of Jordan and the inheritance of the priestly tribe of Levi, which received scattered cities throughout the land (13:8-32; 14:3-4). In this way it is emphasized that all twelve tribes received their inheritances as a unified nation. Together they conquered the land under Joshua's leadership, and together they accepted the portions that God gave them in the land.

The Move to Shiloh (18:1-2)

Up to this time the base camp for the Israelites had been at Gilgal near the Jordan. From there Joshua had conducted the military campaigns and allotted land to Judah, Ephraim, and Manasseh. Now the "whole congregation" moved to Shiloh, a city in the territory assigned to Ephraim about twenty miles north of Jerusalem (v. 1; cf. 16:6). There in Shiloh Joshua set up the "tabernacle of meeting," also called the "tent of meeting" or the "tabernacle." It was the portable place of worship that the Israelites carried with them through the wilderness. The tabernacle itself has not been mentioned since the Lord commissioned Joshua to become Israel's leader in place of Moses (Deut. 31:14-15), although the ark of the covenant figured prominently in chapters 3, 4 and 6 of Joshua. It is possible that a reference to it occurs when Joshua used the term "house of the LORD" in connection with God's treasury in Gilgal (6:24).

Shiloh became the center of worship for the Israelites in their new land for the next four hundred years, until David became king and brought the ark of the covenant to Jerusalem. Moses had repeatedly warned them of the danger of adopting the idol worship of the Canaanites and revering the places where it was practiced. He told them to "cut down the carved images of their gods and

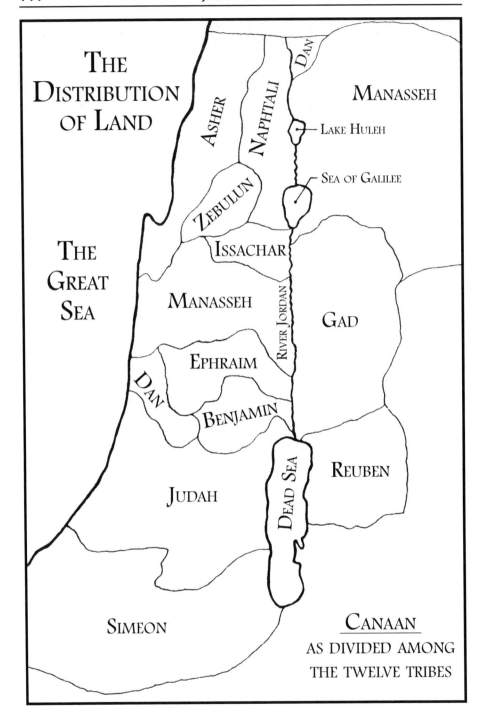

destroy their names from that place" (Deut. 12:3). He also told them that God would choose a place in the land in which to place His Name, and they were to worship Him there (Deut. 12:5). Shiloh means "peace" or "rest"—an apt name bearing in mind that God had given them rest. The Israelites were able to move to Shiloh with Joshua because "the land was subdued before them" (v. 1), which meant that Canaanite military opposition from the major cities had been defeated.

A Rebuke from Joshua (18:2-4)

Joshua assembled the people at Shiloh and reminded them that seven tribes had not yet received their inheritance. It appears that they were in no hurry to be assigned a section of land for which they had to fight alone. Maybe they did not have enough faith to believe that God would actually help them to claim it. It was one thing to be united with their fellow Israelites and be led by Joshua to whom God actually spoke; it was another thing to "go it alone" in facing the enemies remaining in Canaan. They held back. Therefore Joshua chided them, "How long will you neglect to go and possess the land which the LORD God of your fathers has given you?" (v. 3).

Joshua again touches on a theme that runs through the book regarding the fact that God had already *given* them their inheritance (cf. 1:2, 6; 2:24; 6:2; 8:1; 10:8; 15:19). If they did not actively accept and take possession of it, it demonstrated their lack of faith and their lack of thankfulness. In the light of all God had done in their history they should have moved forward with confidence in God. But they did not possess the faith in God that Caleb had when he had requested Hebron for an inheritance, and that especially *because* it contained walled cities and was defended by giants (14:10-12). For this reason Joshua prodded them into taking action. He told the seven tribes to each pick out three men from their tribe and he would send these twenty-one representatives throughout all the remaining land to survey the land and its cities.

The Land is Divided Before the Lord (18:5-7)

When the chosen representatives had finished their survey they were to divide the surveyed land into seven more or less equal parts and return with the results to Joshua in Shiloh. How much resistance the twenty-one representatives might have encountered while conducting their survey is unknown. Joshua told the representatives that both Judah's assigned inheritance to the south and Joseph's inheritance in the north would remain intact (v. 5). When they returned, Joshua said he would assign the portions by casting lots "before the LORD," that is, in His presence (v. 6). They would gather before the "tabernacle of *meeting*" (emphasis added; cf. v. 1) where the ark of the covenant stood, which symbolized God's presence with them. The significance of the Lord's presence in the selection process was that they could be assured that each lot chosen would be His choice for that tribe (v. 6).

Joshua concluded his remarks by reminding them that the tribe of Levi was to have no land inheritance. Rather, their inheritance was to be "the priesthood of the Lord" (v. 7). Earlier, their inheritance was said to be comprised of "the sacrifices of the Lord God of Israel" (13:14), and "the Lord God of Israel" Himself (13:33). All three phrases indicate that theirs was primarily a spiritual inheritance. Joshua also reminded them of another fact they knew well: that Moses had previously given the inheritances to the 2½ tribes on the east side of Jordan. Together with the inheritance of Judah, Ephraim and the other half of Manasseh already allotted on the west side all the tribes were provided for.

The Land Surveyed (18:8-10)

The twenty-one men performed their task and "wrote the survey in a book in seven parts" (v. 9). We presume that they selected seven portions of equal size and value so that the allotment would be viewed as fair to all seven tribes. With their results written and settled, little room would be left for quibbling. When they had brought them back to Joshua, he cast lots for each of the tribes, and they received their inheritances preserving their unity as a nation. Once more we read that it was done "before the Lord."

The descriptions for each tribe are those listed in chapters 18 and 19. The main points of interest of each one will be selected without attempting a detailed analysis. We should bear in mind that the biblical record of the borders of each tribe testifies to God's faithfulness in keeping His promises made as far back as Genesis 12. Not every place mentioned is known today, but enough of them are still known to verify that the borders of each tribe align with those of the neighboring tribe. Thus, they can be discerned on a map with reasonable accuracy.

Benjamin's Inheritance (18:11-28)

Benjamin received the first lot which was located "between the children of Judah and the children of Joseph" (v. 11). Being located between these larger tribes gained them some prestige. They were also in the very center of the country. The boundary description for Benjamin begins at its northeast corner at the River Jordan not far from Jericho. From there it continued westward about half way to the Mediterranean Sea. Near Beth Horon it turned southward along its western boundary to a point near Kirjath Jearim (v. 14). The southern border is described from that point eastward toward Jerusalem where considerable detail is recorded (vv. 15-17), as almost every place name is repeated from the northern boundary description of Judah (15:5-11). Then it continued on eastward to the northern end of the Salt Sea (vv. 18-20). The eastern border consisted of a short section along the Jordan. A list of Benjamin's cities is also given. Twelve of them were in the eastern portion, fourteen others were in the western portion (vv. 21-28).

Simeon's Inheritance (19:1-9)

The second lot was Simeon's. His portion was inside Judah's allotment, which had already proved to be "too much for them" (v. 9). Therefore, Joshua's delegation had apparently selected a part of the southern section of Judah's inheritance as one of the seven portions to be given to the remaining seven tribes. Thus, a number of cities and their surrounding areas were selected in the southern part of Judah as the portion which became Simeon's lot. Nothing but desert lay south of the cities assigned to Simeon. Effectively Simeon became the southernmost of the twelve tribal territories. Whether Simeon was independent of Judah, or was to some degree controlled by Judah, is not stated, but the fact that no boundary points are mentioned, and only city names are given, makes it appear that Simeon inherited the cities but was otherwise subservient to and worked together with Judah (Judg. 1:3).

The reason for Simeon's scattered cities in Judah would seem to be tied to the prophecy concerning him made by Jacob on his death-bed. Simeon, along with his younger brother Levi, had instigated a terrible massacre in the city of Shechem (Gen. 34:24-30). Because of this, Jacob had prophesied of them, "I will divide them in Jacob and scatter them in Israel" (Gen. 49:7). This prophecy was fulfilled by both tribes being scattered among the others. Levi, however, was certainly favored more than Simeon, the reasons for which we shall consider in chapter 21.

Simeon's cities are listed in two groups. In the first there were thirteen cities (vv. 2-6), of which most were included among the cities of Judah listed in chapter 15. Of them, Beersheba, the city of the patriarchs, is the best known (Gen. 22:19; 26:23; 46:1). In later times, however, it is listed as a city of Judah (1 Kings 19:3). In the second group, four cities, two of them in the Negev and two in the Shephelah (or foothills) are mentioned with associated villages surrounding them (vv. 7-8).

Zebulun's Inheritance (19:10-16)

The third lot cast by Joshua fell to the tribe Zebulun, whose inheritance was located in the north of the country in the hills overlooking the Valley of Jezreel. A general boundary description is given, although it is impossible to trace accurate lines. At no point did Zebulun's territory touch the sea even though their inheritance was connected with the sea in two earlier references (Gen. 49:13; Deut. 33:18-19). The passages indicate that Zebulun's future prosperity was to be connected with fishing and maritime commerce. One possible explanation might be that they were positioned near the trade route from the port city of Acco to the military stronghold of Megiddo. They may therefore have had commercial connections. One more problem exists, in that although five cities are named in the list, the total is given as twelve (v. 15). Interestingly, Nazareth is not mentioned, despite the fact that it was located within Zebulun's boundaries.

Issachar's Inheritance (19:17-23)

Issachar's territory included the eastern part of the Valley of Jezreel and the sparsely populated hills to the south. It reached from its common border on the west with Zebulun to the River Jordan on its eastern border. Three cities are mentioned in connection with the boundary and thirteen more cities are listed within its territory, making a total of sixteen (v. 22). Jezreel, Mount Tabor, and Shunem are well known biblical sites, but more than half of Issachar's cities are mentioned nowhere else in Scripture, so their exact locations are not known.

Asher's Inheritance (19:24-31)

Asher's territory was in the northwestern corner of the land. It ran along the Mediterranean Sea from Mount Carmel in the south to the city of Sidon in the north. Its eastern border was common with Zebulun and Naphtali. From a strategic perspective Asher was in an important position because it included the well-known coastal ports of Acco, Tyre and Sidon, and four other coastal cities. However, Asher was unable to take these cities. Thus, they "dwelt among the Canaanites of the land; for they did not drive them out" (Judg. 1:31-32).

Naphtali's Inheritance (19:32-39)

The sixth lot went to Naphtali, which included the heartland of Galilee with its forests and hills. Asher's territory was to the west, and its eastern border went from the Sea of Galilee northward along the upper Jordan. For the first time in these lists, some of the cities are described as being "fortified" (v. 35). This cannot mean that they were the only cities fortified in Canaan, for there were many. We assume that this is the only place where the author includes the information. Not all the cities mentioned can be located, especially those in the north.

Dan's Inheritance (19:40-48)

The last of the seven lots went to Dan. This portion of land lay west of Benjamin in the narrow strip between Judah on the south and Ephraim and Manasseh on the north. It was the northern end of the country occupied by the Philistines. No boundaries are given, only a list of cities. Dan failed to take these cities, or even to move into their allotted inheritance. Instead, the Danites moved north into upper Galilee, took possession of the city of Leshem, and settled there (v. 47; cf Judg. 1:34). This important city they later renamed Dan (v. 47). It became the northern limit of the land of Israel. Israel's territory was later described from north to south as being from "Dan to Beersheba" (Judg. 20:1). In biblical history Dan is best known as one of the two cities where King Jeroboam erected a golden calf to keep the northern kingdom of Israel from going to Jerusalem to worship God there (1 Kings 12:29-30).

Joshua's Inheritance (19:49-51)

The distribution of the land of Canaan west of the Jordan was all but complete. It had begun with Caleb's personal request for the city of Hebron (14:12-15) and it ends on a similar note with Joshua making a personal request for a city in Ephraim called Timnath Serah, probably located in Ephraim's hill country about fifteen miles southwest of Shechem (v. 50). We learn later that he was buried there (24:30). The personal inheritances of Joshua and Caleb are like bookends at either end of the distribution of the entire land of Canaan. Joshua and Caleb had been the two spies who had the faith and courage to recommend that the Israelites move in to take the land God had promised them. For their courage, God had not only preserved them alive to take part in the conquest of Canaan, but had promised them a personal inheritance in the land.

In Conclusion

Verse 51 concludes the distribution of land to the seven remaining tribes by repeating all its essential details. The place where the lots were drawn was Shiloh. The main parties involved in the process were "Eleazer the priest, Joshua the son of Nun, and the heads of the fathers of the tribes of the children of Israel." The method of distributing the land among the seven tribes was by "lot." Finally, it was all done in the presence of God, which is indicated by doing it "before the LORD" and "at the door of the tabernacle of meeting." It was in the place of God's choice, overseen by the leaders, and ordained by God. It was accomplished by faith, without human manipulation, and done in the consciousness of God's presence with them. These principles can be most instructive to Christian leaders in every age.

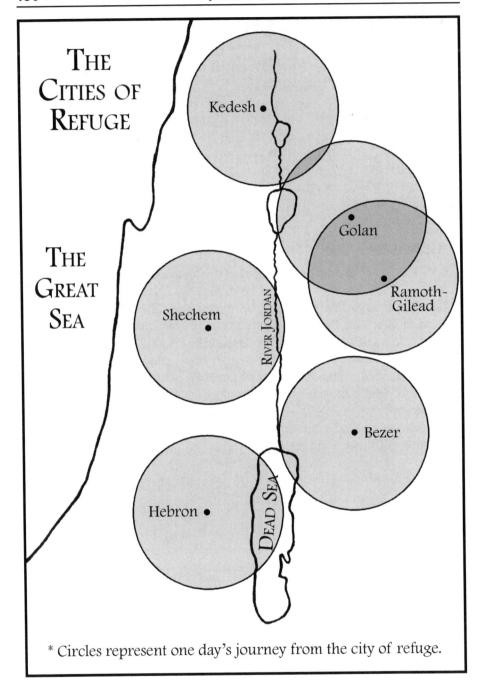

Joshua 20

The Cities of Refuge

With the exception of Levi, every tribe of Israel had received their allotment in the land. The Levites had been chosen by God for priestly duties and would not receive a land allotment. Instead, they were assigned forty-eight cities throughout the land (chapter 21) in which to live. Six of these Levitical cities were also designated as "cities of refuge," or cities of asylum, for the purpose of preserving the sanctity of human life in Israel.

The importance of these cities to the young nation beginning their national life in the Promised Land should not be missed. After several years of war with the Canaanites during which God had instructed the Israelites to utterly destroy them and drive them out, it would have been easy for the Israelites to conclude that God considered human life to be relatively cheap. The truth brought out in this chapter is the very opposite: human life is indeed most precious to God and was to be preserved in the new nation with great care. Any regression toward the "law of the jungle," particularly the unlawful shedding of blood, would actually defile the land God had given them (Num. 35:33-34). As blood revenge was widely practiced in those times, God ordered Israel to set up cities of refuge in order to protect and preserve life. They were to be cities with walls to protect those who belonged inside and to keep out those who did not belong.

The Background to Cities of Refuge

Biblical references to the establishment of cities of refuge are found in four passages in the Pentateuch. The first is in Exodus 21:12-14 following the giving of the Ten Commandments. It begins by stating that anyone who committed premeditated murder would "surely be put to death." A murderer would not be allowed to live in Hebrew society because human life is precious and the taking of it is a serious sin. As a capital offense it would result in capital punishment. However, if someone died as the result of an accident ("If he did not lie in wait") Moses promised, "I will appoint for you a place where he may flee." The reason behind this escape clause for the unintentional killer was that *his* life was also precious.

The second passage (in Numbers 35) designated that three cities of refuge were to be selected on the east side of the Jordan and three in the land of

Canaan itself (Num. 35:14). Anyone who accidentally killed another person could flee to one of these cities to find refuge there, at least until he "stands before the congregation in judgment" (Num. 35:15). The rest of that chapter explains in detail the difference between murder (deliberate premeditated killing) and manslaughter (unintended killing).

The third passage is found in Deuteronomy 4:41-43, written after the 2½ tribes had been allotted the land east of the Jordan. It reports that Moses obeyed the Lord by setting apart three cities of refuge in the area east of Jordan—Bezer, Ramoth, and Golan.

In the fourth passage (also in Deuteronomy), Moses provided more specific instructions about those three cities (Deut. 19:1-13). The cities were to be clearly marked and roads were to be built to aid the refugee in getting there quickly. Moses also gave an example of what is meant by unintentional killing—that of a woodsman's ax head slipping off and killing his neighbor. That man, said Moses, was "not worthy of death, since he had not hated the victim in time past" (Deut. 19:6). He could run for safety to one of the cities of refuge, "lest innocent blood be shed in the midst of your land" (Deut. 19:10). However, if it was murder, there would be no sanctuary for him. "The elders of his city shall send and bring him from there, and deliver him over to the hand of the avenger of blood, that he may die" (Deut. 19:12).

The Need For Cities of Refuge

In the Old Testament world, when someone killed a family member, whether or not the killing was intentional, the family of the victim would gather together and designate one of them to be an "avenger of blood." It was his familial and social duty to track down and avenge the death of their relative to "put away the guilt of innocent blood from Israel" (Deut. 19:13). The practice provided a measure of quick and primitive justice if the killing was deliberate, but if it was accidental, there was potential for great injustice. God designated certain cities as places of refuge for several reasons:

- ➢ To give the accused person an opportunity to defend himself before the elders and to establish that his act was manslaughter, not first degree murder. His life would be preserved, but he would be required to remain in the city of refuge. In this way the sanctity of the unintentional killer's life was maintained.
- ➢ To give the avenger an opportunity to make his case if he thought the refugee was guilty of first-degree murder. If the elders found him guilty, he would be handed over to the avenger of blood for execution. In this case the sanctity of the victim's life was the issue.
- ➢ To provide a form of punishment for the one guilty of manslaughter, whose safety now depended on staying in the city of refuge. He was

actually an exile. Having to stay in exile highlighted the seriousness of the loss of life with which he was associated.
- ➢ To provide a means by which people unrelated to the victim or to the accused could establish the truth about the intent, motive, and instrument used in the killing.

The entire process served as a warning to all the people. Basically, they were to avoid endangering human life in any way because it is sacred. They were not to deliberately take a life and they were to take pains to not accidentally take someone's life. In the example Moses used, when the woodcutter understood the sanctity of human life, he was responsible to examine the condition of his ax if his neighbor was anywhere in the vicinity and be sure that the head of his ax was firmly attached to the handle. His responsibility was to not endanger his neighbor. If he did, he was still guilty of a crime, though lesser than first-degree murder. Though the death was an accident, there would still be consequences. With these passages in mind, we shall turn to our study in Joshua 20.

Appointing Cities of Refuge (vv. 1-3)

Joshua 20 complements the previous teaching concerning the cities of refuge and puts it in the context of the social life of the children of Israel in their newly conquered land. In this passage the Lord told Joshua that he was to instruct the Israelites to appoint or designate the cities of refuge which they had previously been told about through Moses. They needed to appoint three more cities of refuge, these on the west of the Jordan.

God repeated to Joshua the purpose of these cities. They were to be a refuge for the person who had accidentally killed another person and was being pursued by an avenger of blood. The avenger was usually the nearest male relative of the victim, and may possibly have had to be approved by the elders of the city where the accident had taken place. The avenger's job was to avenge the blood of the victim, not to distinguish between accidental manslaughter and deliberate murder. That distinction was to be made by the elders of the city of refuge to which the accused might flee.

Approaching a City of Refuge (vv. 4-6)

The one who had killed his neighbor would have been in a desperate hurry to get to the nearest city of refuge, for the avenger of blood would have been right behind him. To help him, Moses had told the people to "prepare roads" to the cities (Deut. 19:3). Jewish commentators tell us that they made the roads wide, kept them in good repair, bridged streams, and removed obstructions. At the crossroads and corners they put up large lettered signs—REFUGE—so that the desperate runner would not miss his way.

The Lord explained to Joshua the way in which an accused killer needed to approach a city of refuge. When he arrived he was to stand at the entrance of the gate of the city, where that the elders of any ancient walled city met to conduct city affairs and business. He was to present his case to the elders, who would presumably hold a preliminary hearing to satisfy themselves that the case was worthy of their attention. They then would "give him a place," that is, they would assign him somewhere to stay in the city until the case could be considered carefully and witnesses could be called (v. 4).

The avenger of blood, when he appeared, would demand that the elders hand over the accused for execution. If the accused claimed the killing had been accidental the elders would refuse to hand him over until a formal hearing could be conducted. He would be summoned to stand "before the congregation for judgment" (v. 6). It is not explicitly stated whether the hearing would have been conducted only in the city of refuge or, as seems more likely, also in the city where the killing took place (v. 6, 9; cf. Num. 25:24-25; Deut. 19:12).

If the accused was found guilty of premeditated murder, he would be handed over to the avenger of blood. If guilty only of manslaughter, he could remain safely in the city of refuge until the death of the high priest. However, if he left the city and was discovered, the avenger of blood could legally kill him. Perhaps an illustration of this can be gleaned from the story of Abner who had formerly been King Saul's general and had gone over to David's side after Saul's death. In the heat of a chase he had killed Asahel, the brother of David's general, Joab. No malice or forethought was involved. Abner then ran for Hebron, a city of refuge. Joab became the avenger of blood. He pursued Abner as far as the gate of Hebron. Abner would have been secure if he had entered the city, but Joab found him at the gate and killed him. How foolish he was! David lamented Abner's death and said that he had died as a fool dies (2 Sam. 2:23; 3:23-30, 33).

The Death of the High Priest (v. 6)

The amount of time the manslayer was required to remain in exile in the city of refuge was determined by how long the then-serving high priest remained alive. He was free to return to his home only after the death of the high priest. Some question arises as to the significance of the death of the high priest. Some commentators see it only as a convenient terminal point (or amnesty period) for the manslayers who were confined in the cities of refuges. Other commentators, both Christian and Jewish, see significance in the fact that the high priest was God's anointed mediator. Numbers 35:25, which is a parallel passage, particularly describes the high priest as the one "anointed with oil." In this context His anointing as high priest would not mean anything if his death simply marked a point in time.

The high priest's anointing with holy oil signified the presence of the Holy Spirit who empowered him to represent the nation on the Day of Atonement to make amends for the sin of the people. It is therefore thought that, since his life and work were representative in nature, his death might also be representative as a death for the sins of the manslayer. The manslayer's sin could now be regarded as atoned for, allowing him to return to his home as an accepted member of his community. If this view is correct, it pictures the work of the Lord Jesus Christ, our High Priest who, "through the eternal Spirit offered Himself without spot to God," to accomplish our eternal redemption and deliverance (Heb. 9:14-15).

The Six Cities of Refuge (vv. 7-10)

The Israelites on the west side of the Jordan then appointed three cities to be designated as cities of refuge: Kedesh in the north, Shechem in the center, and Hebron in the south (v. 7). They also re-designated the three cities already assigned on the east side (v. 8). Their locations were chosen so that they would be as accessible as possible to as many people as possible as quickly as possible. Each one stood on elevated land so they would be visible. All three in the "west" were associated with mountains (v. 7), while those in the "east" had names that mean elevated. The Jews say that the gates of these cities were open both day and night to assist the accused person. The six cities of refuge would be available to all people, not just Jews, living or visiting among the Israelites. Any accused killer could ask for asylum until he "stood before the congregation" (v. 9). This equality of including justice for all was a radical departure from the practice of the other nations in that it reflected the wisdom, justice, and compassion of God rather than the unfair and heartless mind of man. The whole system was a wonderful provision.

Shadows of New Testament Truth in the Cities of Refuge

The cities of refuge point to at least two areas of truth in the New Testament that are worthy of consideration. The seeker of refuge is seen by many to picture the nation Israel, who killed their Messiah, not fully aware of the enormity of their sin. In at least one sense the nation did not know what they were doing (Luke 23:34; cf. Acts 3:17), yet one day they will realize what they have done and in repentance will run to find refuge in their Messiah (Isa. 53; Zech. 12:10). In that day He will forgive their sin and receive them as His own.

The seeker of refuge may also picture the individual sinner who is guilty before God and acknowledges that he is undeserving of salvation while admitting that he cannot save himself. He is constantly and relentlessly being pursued by an avenger—the righteous judgment of an offended God. In his desperation the sinner hears of a place of refuge in Christ. He believes the message and runs to Christ his Refuge, where he finds safety and security. The author of Hebrews seems to allude to this thought when he says that the believer in Christ has "strong consolation" because he has "fled for refuge, to lay hold of the hope set before us" (Heb. 6:18). Thus in Christ we have refuge from the storm of God's judgment, refuge from the Accuser, refuge from the condemnation that our sinfulness has brought upon us. We can say with the psalmist that "God is our refuge" (Ps. 46:1). How many people remain outside the security found in Christ and will die, as Abner did, like fools, because they have not fled for refuge to Him!

Just as the cities of refuge were sited on elevated locations, making them clearly visible, so the Son of Man was "lifted up" on the cross to draw all people to Him (John 12:32). He told Nicodemus that he would be lifted up for all to see, just as Moses had lifted up the serpent in the wilderness (John 3:14). The cleared and signposted roads made access the city of refuge accessible to all in the same way that access to Christ is available to all who want to come to Him. As the gates of the city of refuge were open all the time and to anyone, whether Jew or Gentile, rich or poor, citizen or alien, so the Bible says that anyone who comes will never be turned away, and that once inside there is perfect safety for all who enter.

In Conclusion

Even the meanings of the names of the six cities seem to confirm what the believer enjoys when he or she finds refuge in Christ. Kadesh means "holy" or "sanctuary," which reminds us that we find sanctuary in Christ Himself. Shechem means "shoulder" or "strength," and isn't it true that we find strength in Him! He is the Lord who will carry the government of the world one day on one shoulder. He is also the Good Shepherd who carries His sheep on His shoulders (plural). Hebron means "fellowship" or "communion," which speaks of our communion with Him. Bezer means "fortified place" or "safety," and in Christ we have a Strong Tower. Ramoth means "height," and the believer is raised up with Christ in the heavenlies. Golan means "exultation" and may speak of the joy of those who are secure in Christ. Christ is thus revealed in all the names of the cities of refuge.

> How firm a foundation, ye saints of the Lord,
> Is laid for your faith in his excellent Word!
> What more can we say than to you He hath said,
> To you who for refuge to Jesus have fled?
>
> Rippon's Selection of Hymns

JOSHUA 21

The Levitical Cities

Chapter 21 is the last of nine chapters devoted to the inheritances that the tribes and some individuals received in the Promised Land. Long before the Israelites had invaded the land, God told them through Moses to assign the Levites certain cities belonging to the other tribes in which they could live. Not only were they to live in those cities, but they were to have the use of common land surrounding those cities as pasture for their flocks (Num. 35:1-3). The common ground for pasture was to stretch two thousand cubits outside the city in all four directions (Num. 35:5).

The Levites' Inheritance

The Levites were the tribe assigned to be the priests and the religious workers, leaders, and teachers. Their inheritance provided them with cities throughout Israel in which to live and serve God among the people. Their priestly and religious service was to be centered in those cities. Because of this responsibility they were to look beyond the material blessings of the land and to see the Lord as their inheritance. Their spiritual inheritance had been made clear to them by Moses and Joshua on five previous occasions (Num. 18:20; Deut. 10:9; 18:2; Josh. 13:33; 18:7). Believers in the church today all belong to a holy priesthood which offers up spiritual sacrifices acceptable to God (1 Peter 2:5). We are heirs to a wonderful spiritual inheritance as well that most of us do not appreciate enough (Eph. 1:11, 14).

The Claim of the Levites (vv. 1-3)

Shiloh had become the political and religious center of life in the Promised Land. It was there that the tribal leaders of Levi approached Eleazar the priest, Joshua the son of Nun, and the fathers of the tribes of the children of Israel to make their claim (Num. 35:1-8). The rulers from the other tribes quickly agreed that the claim was fair and legitimate as the "commandment of the Lord". Thus, the request was readily granted (v. 3).

The Four Levite Groups Receive their Cities by Lot (vv. 4-8)

Joshua begins by summarizing the allocation of the cities in four groups. Lots were used once again to ensure that it was God who made the selections, not a powerful group or an individual. The Levites were divided into four groups according to the descendants of the three sons of Levi. Each group was allotted cities in three tribal areas. The first group was descended from Levi's son Kohath through Aaron. These Aaronic Kohathites received thirteen cities in the tribal areas of Judah, Simeon, and Benjamin (v. 4). The second group consisted of all the other Kohathites who received ten cities in Ephraim, Dan, and the half-tribe of Manasseh on the western side of the Jordan (v. 5). The third group of Levites included those descended from Levi's son Gershon. They were allocated thirteen cities in the tribal areas of Issachar, Asher, Naphtali, and the half of Manasseh that was in Bashan east of the Jordan (v. 6). The fourth group included those descended from Levi's son Merari. They were allocated twelve cities located in the tribal areas of Reuben, Gad, and Zebulun (v. 7). In this way the Levites received forty-eight cities and their pasturelands scattered all over Israel. All this was to fulfill the command of the LORD to Moses (Num. 35:2).

The Names of the Levitical Cities (vv. 9-42)

Having summarized the four groups of Levites and the tribal areas where the cities had been allocated for each of the groups, Joshua now lists the names of the cities assigned by lot to each of these same groups. The names follow the same order as in the summary beginning with the Aaronites (vv. 9-19), followed by the other Kohathites (vv. 20-26), then the Gershonites (vv. 27-33), and finally the Merarites (vv. 34-40). For the purposes of this commentary, remarking on each of the names will not be necessary.

Some observations, however, may be helpful. First, among these Levitical cities were all six of the cities of refuge. This gave the refugees an opportunity to have religious as well as political help in seeking asylum. Second, a good number of these cities had not yet been subdued and did not come into Israel's hands for some time, for example, Gezer (1 Kings 9:16) and Taanach (Judges 1:37). Third, the cities assigned to the Aaronites were strategically located close to Jerusalem where the temple would ultimately be built. God had arranged that the priests would be nearest the temple and in the southern kingdom of Judah, which would survive 136 years longer than the northern kingdom.

God Fulfills His Promise (vv. 43-45)

The last three verses in chapter 21 conclude the section of Joshua dealing with the distribution of the land (chapters 13-21). These nine chapters are the heart of the book because they show that God's promises to the patriarchs to give their descendants the land were fulfilled to the letter. God had made it possible for Israel to cross the Jordan, conquer the enemy, possess the land, apportion it into twelve tribal sections, and establish a center for worship and a means for continued religious instruction. Their victory was complete. In recognition of the Lord's enabling, Joshua gives us this summary as an expression of praise to God for His faithfulness.

God Gifts Them the Land (v. 43)

The first note of praise acknowledged that the land was a gift from God. The gift had been promised by oath to their "fathers" starting with Abraham, to whom God had said, "I give it to you" (Gen. 13:17; 17:8). God's gift of the land has also been stressed in the book of Joshua starting with His promise to him in the second verse and reiterated no less than thirty times (1:2). Our verse summarizes, "So the Lord gave to Israel all the land of which He had sworn to give to their fathers." The second note of praise was that the Israelites "took possession of" and "dwelt in" the land that God had given them. They had actively received God's gift in possessing it by conquest and then enjoyed the benefit of it by settling in its cities and farming its land. They had advanced from owning nothing but a small cemetery in the land (Genesis 23) to the point where they could settle down in it as a nation and enjoy it.

God Gives Them Rest (v. 44)

The third note of praise in these summary verses is that God gave them rest in the land as He had promised. When God told Moses to lead the people from Mount Sinai to give them the "land which I swore to Abraham," He also had said, "My Presence will go with you, and I will give you rest" (Ex. 33:1, 14). The theme of rest as a promise connected with the land continued in the farewell messages of Moses just before he died (Deut. 3:20; 12:9-10; 25:19). Joshua then picks up the theme of the promise of rest for Israel in chapter 1 (1:13, 15). He states in his summary that the rest God had promised was now an accomplished fact; "The Lord gave them rest all around according to all that He had sworn to their fathers."

The fourth note of praise was that God had defeated their enemies. Their rest in the land was closely associated with defeating their enemies: "Not a man of all their enemies stood against them; the Lord delivered all their enemies into their hand" (v. 44). Early in the conquest, when they had been defeated at Ai, Joshua had been afraid that the promise would not be fulfilled. But when they trusted in God, neither the coalitions of Canaanites in the south or in the north were able to stand against them (chapters 10-11). This is exactly what God had promised Joshua from the beginning (1:5).

Not a Word Failed (v. 45)

The final note of praise is that not one word from God had "failed" (lit. "fell to the ground"). Every word God had "spoken to the house of Israel" had been fulfilled. The term "house of Israel" refers to the unity of the twelve tribes, for God had made the promises He had now fulfilled to all twelve of the tribes together.

The reader should understand that these three verses about God's fulfillment of every promise are to be understood as part of a two-sided tapestry. On one side is Joshua's sweeping conquest of the land as pictured here, and on the other side there is a story of incomplete conquest and much land that remained to be possessed (13:2-6). Judah had failed to drive out the Jebusites from Jerusalem (15:63). Ephraim had failed to drive out the Canaanites from Gezer (16:10), and Manasseh had failed to take several towns (17:12). Between the broad conquests and the obvious failures there is constant tension in the book. This tension should not surprise the believer who in his or her spiritual life enjoys the sweeping victory that our greater Joshua (Jesus) has won on our behalf and also experiences failure to possess and enjoy all that God has intended in Christ (Eph. 1:11).

In Conclusion

Chapter 21 provides some excellent lessons in the provision God made for the Levites as the worship leaders and teachers of the Law. By uniformly scattering them among all the tribes, God ensured all Israel would have access to spiritual counsel and good teaching. Note also that God made provision for the material welfare of those who spent themselves for the spiritual needs of the people. They were given cities to live in and pasture lands for their flocks. Still today God provides for the spiritual edification of His people (Eph. 4:11-12) and the material needs of His workers.

JOSHUA 22

A Crisis Averted

Chapter 22 turns our attention to the 2½ tribes whose homes were on the east side of the Jordan. After about seven years of fighting alongside their brethren, they were going home. Joshua called them together at Shiloh to release them from their obligations and to bid them farewell. He assumed the role of a priestly patriarchal father to bless them, provide for them, and instruct them. In sending them away Joshua wanted to maintain the unity of the nation, because living east of the Jordan would make it harder for them to maintain close contact with those on the west side. Any people or group on the fringe is always the most vulnerable to the danger of drifting away or becoming independent of the whole.

Joshua Congratulates the Eastern Tribes (vv. 1-3)

Joshua congratulated them for obeying "all that Moses the servant of the LORD commanded" them (v. 2). Moses had commanded the 2½ tribes, "you shall pass before your brethren armed, all your mighty men of valor, and help them, until . . . they also have taken possession of the land which the Lord your God is giving them. Then you shall return to the land of your possession and enjoy it" (1:14-15). They had not only done this, but for about seven years had also "obeyed" Joshua's "voice" (v. 2). Note how their obedience to Moses' command and to Joshua's voice is the same. Joshua's leadership was an extension of Moses' leadership.

Joshua went on to say that they had kept the charge that the Lord had given them (v. 3). It was a wonderful commendation to the 2½ tribes that they had completed all that they had been charged to do, even though it took "many days," that is, years, of struggle. Their faithfulness over the "long haul" reminds us of Paul's statement at the end of his life when he reviewed his life as a believer: "I have fought the good fight . . . I have kept the faith" (2 Tim. 4:7).

God's Faithfulness and Their Responsibility (vv. 4-5)

Joshua reminded them that God too had been faithful in keeping His promise to give rest to their brethren. Therefore, Joshua commanded them, "Go . . . to the land of your possession," another term for their inheritance. Once there, however, they were not to relax in their obedience to God. Joshua instructed them, "take careful heed to do the commandment and the law which Moses the servant of the LORD commanded you" (v. 5). These words echoed the words of God to Joshua before the conquest (1:7). Thus, what God had commanded Joshua to do in chapter 1, Joshua now commanded these to do. They would enjoy rest in the land of their inheritance only if they continued to keep the law and commandments of Moses.

Five Commands (v. 5)

Joshua summarized what these commandments were with five key phrases taken from Moses' writings in Deuteronomy.

- ➢ They were to "love the LORD," which was the first and greatest commandment (Deut. 6:5; Matt. 22:37).
- ➢ They were to "walk in all His ways," indicating that people made in God's image should act as He would (Deut. 8:6; 10:12; 19:9; 30:16).
- ➢ They were to "keep His commandments" by their obedience to all the statutes and laws that Moses had given them in the wilderness years (Deut. 8:6, 11:1, 30:10, 16).
- ➢ They were to "hold fast to Him" (Deut. 11:22). In times of trial as well times of joy they were to focus on God who cared for them, guided them, loved them, and disciplined them.
- ➢ They were to "serve Him" with all their heart (Deut. 10:12; 11:13).

This language echoes Moses' summary of the Law in Deuteronomy 10:12: "And now Israel, what does the LORD your God require of you, but to fear the LORD your God, to walk in all His ways and to love Him, to serve the LORD your God with all your heart and with all your soul." *Heart* and *soul* are key Bible words reflecting the believer's proper response to God with every fiber of his being. To do something with all your heart is to strongly determine to do it willingly and gladly. To do it with your soul is to involve your entire inner nature and personality. Heart and soul are used together ten times in the book of Deuteronomy as reflected here in Joshua (Deut. 6:5; 10:12; 13:3; 30:2). To fail to apply the heart and the soul to God's service leads to drifting and eventually opens the door of apostasy, both for the ancient Israelites and for us.

Joshua Blesses the Two and a Half Tribes (vv. 6-8)

Joshua now blessed them as they left Shiloh (v. 6). At this point the author interrupts the blessing to restate the situation regarding the inheritance of the tribe of Manasseh (v. 7). He emphasizes the unity of the eastern and western sections of the tribe in light of the strain on that unity that is soon to occur. Thus, Joshua's blessing is interrupted to make this point so that it is not missed.

Along with the blessing they were to receive their share of the spoils of war that had been taken over the past months and years (v. 8). Just as Moses had divided the spoil after the Battle of Midian, Joshua did following the conquest of Canaan (Num. 31:27).

The Perceived Threat to Unity (vv. 9-12)

When the eastern tribes had left with their spoils to return to their homes, they did so with every intention of maintaining unity with their brethren on the west side of Jordan. What happened on their way home precipitated a national crisis that very nearly tore the nation in two before the tribes were even settled on their lands and in their cities. Although the children of Reuben, Gad, and Manasseh thought they were promoting unity by what they did, it was interpreted as a rebellion against the other tribes. To make matters worse, their activities had religious overtones which were taken to mean that they were not only rebelling against their western brothers, but against the Lord. The author's purpose in relating this incident is to warn the nation of the ever-present danger of disunity and idolatry. Indeed these two issues proved over the centuries to be the undoing of the nation.

The Altar Built by the Jordan

The Reubenites, Gadites and one half of the tribe of Manasseh left Shiloh and went east toward the land of Gilead which they had captured and inherited east of the River Jordan. When they came to a place near the river, but still on the western side, they built an altar of stones described as "great" and "impressive" (v. 10). We are not told at this point why they built the altar.

The children of Israel heard that the 2½ tribes had built the altar and "the whole congregation of the children of Israel gathered together at Shiloh to go to war against them" (v. 12). They appeared to believe that the altar presented a grave danger to the unity of the nation if the matter was not resolved. The Israelites assumed that the children of Reuben, Gad, and Manasseh had built an altar without authorization to rival the one Joshua erected in Shiloh (v. 16). The new altar may possible have been in the vicinity of Gilgal where the entire nation had first camped when they first entered the land. It was there that they had kept the feast of the Passover and had established their base camp for the conquest. The children of Israel knew that the Lord had commanded Moses saying that no Israelite could bring an offering anywhere but to the altar at the door of the tabernacle without being "cut off" from His people (Lev. 17:8-9). They knew too that if anyone offered sacrifices to any other gods they should be "utterly destroyed with the edge of the sword" (Deut. 13:15). Under the assumption that one or both of these sins had been committed, the children of Israel began to prepare for war.

The Accusation against the Two and a Half Tribes (vv. 13-20)

The first thing that Israel did was to send representatives to talk to the leaders of the eastern tribes: Phinehas the priest, son of Eleazar and grandson of Aaron, along with ten rulers, one representing each of the 9½ tribes (vv. 13-14). The priest and the ten tribal leaders from Shiloh then met with representatives of the 2½ tribes somewhere in the land of Gilead (v. 15).

The children of Israel represented the "whole congregation of the LORD." They came from Shiloh where the Lord's presence was represented by the tabernacle and accused Reuben, Gad, and Manasseh by asking, "What treachery is this you have committed against the God of Israel, to turn away this day from following the LORD, in that you have built for yourselves an altar, that you might rebel this day against the LORD?" (v. 16). They believed that they had sinned and that their sin constituted a major break in their relationship with God. They feared a swift and devastating judgment from God on the whole nation as a result. By confronting the perceived crisis promptly and openly the children of Israel set us a good example to follow. We should always get the full and true facts before reacting or taking necessary action.

The Example of God's Judgment at Peor (vv. 17-19)

The delegation supported their fear of coming judgment by offering two examples of God's judgment from their own recent experience. The first one they used was what God had done when they had committed the "iniquity of Peor" (v. 17; cf. Num. 25:1-3). God had instructed Moses to hang offenders, then Moses had commanded the judges to execute them. The judges were slow to obey, so God sent a plague among the Israelites in which 24,000 people died (Num. 25:9; Ps. 106:29-30). During the plague, however, a most offensive act was committed at the door of the tabernacle. Phinehas the priest was incensed by this act and killed the offenders by piercing them through with his javelin, after which God stopped the plague (Num. 25:6-9). For Phinehas and the western leaders this was a solemn and serious example that they had observed. Both the root of this rebellion and the stain of its consequences had lasted "until this day" (v. 17). They challenged the children of Reuben, Gad, and Manasseh, "Is the iniquity of Peor not enough . . . that you must turn away this day from following the LORD?" (vv. 17-18). They feared that if the eastern tribes rebelled, God would be angry, and the whole congregation of Israel would then suffer the consequences.

The Example of God's Judgment on Achan's Sin (vv. 19-20)

The western representatives proposed a drastic solution: leave the land of their possession on the east side of the Jordan and move en masse to "the land of the possession of the LORD where the tabernacle stands," on the west side. They believed it would be better to do this than to stay in their land and sink into idolatry. If they became idolaters on the east bank they would then become pagan. The example now used is that of Achan, who in effect became a Canaanite by being unfaithful to the Lord in taking for himself something that the Lord had claimed (7:10-26). Achan's sin is linked to their supposed sin because the word translated "treachery" in verse 16 is translated as "trespass" in verse 20. The result of Achan's sin was that the whole congregation had suffered defeat at Ai.

The Defense of the Accusation (vv. 21-29)

The representatives of the 2½ tribes had heard the accusation of the "heads of the divisions of Israel" and now had opportunity to answer them. Note that it was not Phinehas the priest to whom they spoke, but to the national leaders (v. 21). Their response brought to a climax the whole confrontation, as they declared that they had neither hidden intent nor ill will against their brothers. For the first time we learn that their motives really were truly honorable from the beginning. They were surprised to have been misunderstood and passionately maintained that they always intended to be united with their western brethren and to be faithful to God.

They began by calling God who "knows" the truth as their witness. They used three Hebrew terms for God: *El, Elohim*, and *Yahweh*. Each of these terms is used twice, and the combinations are rendered differently in different English versions (v. 22). They wanted to make it clear that God knew the truth and that all Israel should know it too. The 2½ tribes understood that the western tribes might conclude that, by being in Canaan, they had a stronger claim on God than the eastern tribes did. After all, their inheritance was in Canaan where the tabernacle was located and where the presence of God was manifest. The Jordan River might easily have been seen as a barrier, and those living west of it might conceivably see themselves as being nearer to God.

For this reason the 2½ tribes declared that if any hint of rebellion or treachery or disunity was found in their building of the altar in question, the children of Israel were not to "save" them, but rather destroy them. Furthermore they proclaimed, "If we have built ourselves an altar to turn from following the LORD," no matter what kind of offerings are offered on it, "let the LORD Himself require an account" (v. 23). In other words, whether the children of Israel found them guilty of disunity or God found them guilty of rebellion against Him, they were willing to suffer the just consequences.

They went on to explain the reason for their action, "for fear, for a reason." They were afraid that, in time to come, the descendants of the children of Israel would say to their descendants, "What have you to do with the LORD God of Israel?" (v. 24). They could easily be able to point to the Jordan as a God-made boundary between them and declare to them, "You have no part in the LORD" (v. 25). The end result would likely be that their descendants would stop fearing the Lord. The children of Reuben, Gad, and Manasseh did not want that to happen, so they had devised their plan.

An Altar of Witness (vv. 25-29)

They had decided that they would build an altar, not for sacrifices and offerings, but as a lasting witness, or testimony, between the two sections of the nation. In the same way that a witness in court functions as legal testimony to the truth of a matter, the altar would testify to the truth that the 2½ tribes would join the children of Israel in worshipping at the true altar in Shiloh. There they would perform the service of the Lord with their burnt offerings, sacrifices, and peace offerings (v. 25).

They then gave three further reasons why they should look on it as an altar for witness. First, it stood on the *west* bank of Jordan, where it could hardly have been used as a regular altar of sacrifice for those living across the river (cf. v. 11). Second, they had deliberately made it unnecessarily *large* so that it could be seen from a good distance (cf. v. 10). Third, the altar of witness had been built merely as a *replica* of the true altar at Shiloh. The model, or replica, would stand as an imposing but silent witness between the two groups of Israelites for many generations, rather than as a rival altar of the eastern tribes. They said, "Far be it from us that we should rebel against the LORD, and turn from following the LORD this day" (v. 29). They acknowledged that there was to be no other altar than "the altar of the LORD our God which is before His tabernacle" (v. 29).

The Resolution of the Crisis (vv. 30-34)

Phinehas the priest, with the rulers and the heads of the divisions of the western tribes, heard the defense of the eastern tribes and was pleased. Everyone was entirely satisfied with the explanation of their reasons for building the altar. The serious crisis was over, and the threat to the unity of the twelve tribes was averted. They had been wrong in their assumptions. Now they had the assurance that the Lord was among them in blessing (v. 31). Phinehas and the other representatives of the western tribes then returned home and reported the outcome to the children of Israel who responded with pleasure and blessed God. The altar was named "Witness." It was to "witness" that Yahweh was God, and it would be a perpetual symbol of their unity based on their unique relationship to the covenant God.

In Conclusion

In addition to recognizing the importance of preserving national unity, we learn some practical lesson from this incident. First, we should not discount rumors; we should avoid the folly, however, of jumping to conclusions before ascertaining all the facts of any matter. Second, we should remain calm while we determine the full information and facts so that we do not act precipitously.

Joshua 23

Joshua's Farewell Address to the Leaders

The final two chapters in Joshua contain Joshua's farewell messages to the whole nation of Israel. These messages are similar to the farewell messages of Moses recorded in Deuteronomy. Joshua had been promised the presence of God, just as Moses had. Just as Moses had led the Israelites across the Red Sea, so Joshua led them across the River Jordan. Moses had an encounter with God at the burning bush, and Joshua had a similar encounter before the battle of Jericho. Moses had held up his staff to assure a military victory, just as Joshua held up his javelin to assure victory at Ai. Both men had built altars to the Lord. And now, just as Moses had given his farewell advice to Israel, so Joshua would give similar advice to them following the conquest of Canaan. All these similarities lend weight to the fact that Joshua was considered a worthy successor to Moses.

The Audience of Joshua's Speech at Shiloh

In the absence of any reference to the location for this event, some commentators believe it was Shiloh, where the tabernacle had been set up. It appears to have been primarily addressed to the representatives of the people—the elders, heads, judges, and officers (v. 2). As the leaders of the people they bore a significant responsibility for the nation's on-going fidelity to the Lord. In the first address Joshua focuses on the future, while in the second (recorded in chapter 24) he reminds them of the faithfulness of God in the past. Both of the speeches were given shortly before Joshua's death.

Introduction (vv. 1-2)

A time notation—"a long time after"—introduces Joshua's first speech. Joshua had settled down in his inherited city of Timnath Serah in the hill country of Ephraim (19:49-50). If Joshua had been about the same age as Caleb when they had conquered the land—about 85—and he died at 110, then twenty-five years had elapsed (14:10; 24:29). Twice in these verses we read that Joshua was "old, advanced in age."

The Lord had given rest to Israel. Rest, meaning the end of conflict with their enemies by completing the conquest, has been a theme of the book from the beginning (1:13; 21:44). Rest was a gift from God because it was He who had given them their victories. Without Him there would have been no victories.

Joshua's first message consists of three exhortations, along with several warnings if they did not heed them. All three begin with a reminder of the Lord's faithful acts and end with an exhortation for the people to be faithful to Him. The first exhortation was to completely possess the land and have nothing to do with Canaanite gods (vv. 3-8). The second exhortation was to diligently love the Lord and not intermarry with the Canaanites (vv. 9-13). The third exhortation was to keep the Law and not bow down to idol gods (vv. 14-16), or they would forfeit the land.

Possess the Land (vv. 3-8)

Joshua wanted the leaders to recall the power of the "nations" and the greater power of God in defeating them (v. 3). They had seen God fight for Israel against "all these nations," a term from Deuteronomy used frequently in this chapter but rarely elsewhere. God had not only defeated the nations in Canaan, He had divided up their land by lot to become Israel's inheritance "from the Jordan to the Great Sea westward." In not mentioning the peoples' inheritance east of the Jordan, Joshua did not mean to exclude them; rather he based his speech on the promises of Moses in Deuteronomy. Twenty-five times Moses had promised that Israel would *cross* the Jordan into their new land (Deut. 27:2, 4, 12, etc.). Not only had God driven out the enemies in the past, but He would continue to "expel them" and "drive them out" in order to fulfill His promises (v. 5; Deut. 9:3-5).

In the light of God's fulfilled promises to Israel in the past, Joshua exhorted them, "Therefore be very courageous to keep and to do all that is written in the Book of the Law of Moses" (v. 6), staying on a straight course of consistent obedience. The condition upon which they could keep and enjoy their inheritance was their obedience to the commands of God given through Moses. The "Book of the Law" refers to the inspired writings of Scripture up to that time. The language Joshua used in commanding the people here was the same God had used with him when He had charged him to lead the Israelites across the Jordan (1:7-8).

Israel was told to have nothing to do with the gods of the nations in Canaan. They were to devote themselves to worshiping Yahweh exclusively. Their separation was to be in four areas (v. 7): they were not even to make mention of the names of these gods; they were not to make oaths using their names; they were not to serve them with sacrifices and offerings; and they were not to bow down to them in worship or prayer. To do any of these things would be to recognize these idols as gods and to therefore to deny that the Lord was the only true God.

The importance of this command is clear, especially when we consider that compromising their belief in Yahweh to worship Canaanite gods became their besetting sin throughout their history. Soon after the death of Joshua, they began to serve other gods in the time of the judges (Judg. 2:8-12). Later, the united kingdom under Solomon was split in two by the worship of other gods (1 Kings 11). The northern kingdom made golden calves and was eventually taken into captivity because of their idolatry (2 Kings 17:18). The southern kingdom of Judah also fell into the sin of idolatry and was exiled to Babylon (2 Kings 24:2-3). In light of this danger Joshua told them to "hold fast to the Lord" as they had demonstrated in the incident about the memorial altar (v. 8).

Love the Lord (vv. 9-13)

In the second part of his address Joshua again referenced the past to give a charge concerning the future. He reminded them that the Lord had driven out "great and strong nations" and that "no one has been able to stand against you" (v. 9). On this basis he reasoned, "One man of you shall chase a thousand, for the Lord your God is He who fights for you" (v. 10). His words reflect what Moses had said, "How could one chase a thousand . . . unless . . . the Lord had surrendered them" (Deut. 32:30). This statement was literally fulfilled when Samson took a jawbone and killed a thousand men with it (Judges 15:15-16).

Joshua then challenged the leaders in the light of God's saving actions to diligently love Him. These words echo what Moses had told the Israelites: "Love the Lord your God with all your heart" (Deut. 6:5). The Lord Jesus Christ called this the "first and the greatest commandment" (Matt. 22:37-38). God desired a loving relationship with them that was founded on His faithfulness to them and their loyalty to Him.

Joshua warned in no uncertain terms about the consequences should they fail in their loyalty to God. He began with the alternative to loving God and holding fast, or clinging, to Him (vv. 8-11). They might cling to the nations instead, exemplified by intermarrying with the Canaanite peoples. God had commanded Moses to "take heed . . . lest you make a covenant with the inhabitants of the land . . . lest it be a snare in your midst . . . and you take of his daughters for your sons and his daughters play the harlot with their gods. You shall make no molded gods for yourselves" (Ex. 34:12, 16, 17). In the light of this commandment Joshua was telling them that intermarriage with pagans would certainly lead to the introduction of pagan deities into their lives and homes. The final step would be that they and their children would then worship those idols (v. 12).

If Israel drew back from their love for God in this way, they were to know for certain that God would no longer give them military victories over the nations.

The continued presence of those nations would bring them misery in four ways: They would become *snares* to catch them, *traps* to hold them, *scourges* to punish them and *thorns* to hurt them (v. 13). Joshua repeated to them what Moses told them years before (Num. 33:55; Deut. 7:1-4). But in reality it would not be long until they did exactly what Moses and Joshua had warned them not to do (Judg. 3:1-5). In the New Testament Paul used the story of Israel's entrapment in apostasy and their resulting punishment to warn Christians to stand firm in their faith and to be very careful not to fall into temptation as they did (1 Cor. 10:1-13).

Joshua Exhorts the People to Keep the Covenant (vv. 14-16)

Joshua then exhorted Israel to keep the covenant by which they could live in the land and enjoy God's blessing (v. 16). He told them that he was about to go "the way of all the earth," an expression also used by David that meant to die (1 Kings 2:2). Joshua would no longer be there to lead them, but they knew "in all [their] hearts and in all [their] souls" the absolute certainty of God's faithfulness. Of all the promises God had made to them concerning the conquest of the land, neither "one thing" nor "one word" had failed to come to pass (v. 14; cf. 21:45).

Joshua reasoned that if all the "good things" God had promised had come to pass, then all the "harmful things" about which they had been warned would also come to pass if they transgressed the covenant (v. 16). The covenant was God's contract between Himself and His people. God would bless them as a people in their land with His love, protection, and provision when they obeyed Him. If they disobeyed Him, however, they would experience the curse of His anger, which usually was expressed to Israel by letting them fall into the hands of their enemies. This had happened at Jericho when Achan had stolen the banned items. When they had faced Ai "the Lord's anger burned against the children of Israel" and they were defeated at Ai (7:1). Examples like this one abound in the later history of Israel (Judges 3:8-10:7; 2 Kings 13:3). Joshua warned them that if they disobeyed they would "perish quickly from the good land." The land had been given to them by God and could be taken away by God at His pleasure. Ultimately God did take away the land when first the northern kingdom, and later the southern kingdom, fell into idolatry and rebellion against God. They were defeated by the Assyrians and the Babylonians and taken into exile.

In Conclusion

Perhaps Joshua's first farewell address can be summarized by these three commands: (1) to respond to God by taking the initiative to possess the remaining pockets of land; (2) to love the Lord their God; and (3) to keep the commandments so clearly spelled out in the Book of the Law.

The principles in the challenges and warnings given to Israel apply to us as Christians. Unless we remain steadfastly devoted to God, diligently separating ourselves from the things that would draw us away from Him, we will forfeit the spiritual blessings and victory that God has provided for us in Christ.

Joshua 24

Joshua's Farewell Address to the People

Joshua was now at the end of his life, and he realized that God's purpose for him was accomplished. The land had been partitioned among the tribes with justice for everyone. The spoils of war had been divided fairly among them as well. Unlike most of the victorious generals down through history, Joshua had established a state where all his people shared in the benefits. The reason for this was that Joshua had taken his instructions from God and his goal was to do God's will. He never intended to become a powerful political figure. His aim had simply been to be like his predecessor Moses, God's servant (Deut. 34:5; Josh. 1:2). Here, at the very end of his life, he received the honor of also being called the "servant of the LORD" (v. 29).

The Gathering at Shechem (v. 1)

Joshua's final meeting with the nation occurred at Shechem and was more official than the previous meeting with the leaders at Shiloh. In some ways this speech reflects what Joshua had said to the leaders, but important differences are apparent. The most important one is that chapter 24 includes a ceremony to renew the covenant.

The site for this meeting is significant, for it was at Shechem that God appeared to Abraham and specifically told him that *this* was the land that his descendants would inherit (Gen. 12:6-7). Abraham had built an altar there to demonstrate his faith in God's promise. Many years later Jacob had arrived back in Canaan and had buried the "foreign gods" that his family had brought there from Haran (Gen. 35:4). Shechem was also where Joshua himself had built an altar and had written a copy of the Law of Moses on the stones, after which he read it, with its curses and blessings, to all the congregation as a renewal of the covenant that God had made with them through Moses (8:30-35). Shechem later became one of the cities of refuge (20:7). No doubt the stones on which the blessings and the curses were written were still there when Joshua died. Shechem was, therefore, a most appropriate place for his final words to the nation.

Joshua Reviews Israel's Covenant History (vv. 2-13)

Joshua reviewed Israel's history as a covenant people from the call of Abraham to the conquest of Canaan. He reminded them of their responsibility to fear the Lord and to serve Him alone. The people accepted the terms of the covenant by a firm declaration: "We will serve the LORD." The covenant made at Sinai was not an everlasting covenant; each generation needed to reaffirm it. The renewal of commitment recorded here stands as an example to all God's people today. We, too, need to continually renew our dedication to serve God alone. The gathering at Shechem was more than a meeting to honor Joshua at the end of his life. The tribes of Israel with their elders, heads, judges, and officers "presented themselves before God" (v. 1). They acknowledged that God was among them and that they were ready to listen and respond.

Joshua was the spokesman of God saying, "Thus says the LORD God of Israel." In this way God reminded Israel of the history of their covenant relationship with Him. He began with their ancestors, Terah and two of his sons, Abraham and Nahor, all of whom dwelt on "the other side of the River" (Euphrates), where they served other gods. God said, "I took your father Abraham from the other side of the River and led him throughout all the land of Canaan." In the land, Abraham had many sons, but Isaac was his God-given son of the promise (v. 3). To Isaac God gave Jacob and Esau. To Esau He gave the mountains of Seir (outside the land), but Jacob was not given a land inheritance. Instead he immediately went to Egypt with his family where they grew into a nation. Then God sent Moses and Aaron to His people to deliver them from Egypt. At the Red Sea they had cried out for help when the Egyptian army was pursuing them with chariots and horsemen. God said, "Then your eyes saw what I did in Egypt." Although few of the current nation would have been old enough to recollect much about that time or event (this day being at least sixty five years later), they were still witnesses of God's power.

When they had "dwelt in the wilderness for a long time" God delivered them from the Amorites first, then from the Moabites. Then they had crossed the Jordan, and the seven peoples of Canaan were delivered into their hand (v. 12). God sent the *hornet* before them that drove the enemies out, but "not with your sword or with your bow" (v. 12). The identity of the "hornet" has intrigued commentators. Some have suggested that it speaks of the dread or terror that had gripped the Canaanites before the Israelites invaded. This is confirmed by God's prophecy to Moses in the wilderness that linked together the fear of the Canaanites and hornets (Ex. 23:27-28). Others take the word literally and think that God gathered swarms of hornets to plague the Canaanites as he had done with flies in the plagues of Egypt, but there is no biblical evidence for that. The important point is that their victory was not with human "sword or bow," for God had done it all in His own way. Note the actions of God in verses 3 to 13: "I took . . . I gave . . . I sent . . . I brought . . . I destroyed them . . . I delivered you" etc. Everything was accomplished by God's power, grace, and mercy.

The recounting of God's involvement with His people would have encouraged them. In a similar way, it is good for us to recall how God has been active in our lives. When we do so, it will encourage us to continue to trust Him.

Joshua Rehearses Israel's Responsibilities (vv. 14-24)

In these verses Joshua reviews the stipulations of the covenant. In brief, Israel needed to "fear the LORD" and to "serve the LORD." To do these things they had to reject and renounce all alliances with other gods. There were the gods of their fathers, like the gods Terah had served when he lived beyond the Euphrates River, and there were the gods of the Canaanite people who lived among them. Joshua seems to have assumed that they would choose between the Mesopotamian gods or the Canaanite gods. Whatever their choice would be, he was resolute in *his* choice: "But as for me and my house, we will serve the LORD" (v. 15). Bearing in mind Joshua was close to death, this is a remarkable statement of his determination to be true to the Lord till his dying breath. He spoke for his family as well as for himself. As one of the best-known verses in the Bible, it is a bold statement of his commitment to God, however many days he had left to live. He and Caleb had stood alone before, and he was willing to do it again (Num. 14:1-9).

The people responded to Joshua's arguments and his declaration quickly. "Far be it from us that we should forsake the LORD to serve other gods" (v. 16). They insisted that they would not even entertain the idea. To them it was utterly impossible to imagine that they could be guilty of such ingratitude to God after all He had done for them—the "great signs" and their preservation from enemies along the way. But Joshua did not seem to be satisfied with their expression of faithfulness to God. Perhaps he detected some insincerity in them. His response is most surprising. We might think he would have been delighted with their statement of commitment, but he seems to reject it. He exhorted them, "You cannot serve the LORD for He is a holy God. He is a jealous God; He will not forgive your transgressions nor your sins" (v. 19). Joshua implied that if they forsook God and deliberately served idols it would be a high handed, presumptuous sin for which there was no forgiveness under Mosaic Law (Num. 15:30). However, even after this warning, the people reaffirmed that they would serve the Lord (v. 21).

Joshua spoke to them for a third time, challenging them to be witnesses against themselves that they had chosen to forsake all other gods and serve the Lord (v. 22). He then spoke to them for the fourth and final time and came to the point he had made at the beginning. "Now therefore," he said, "put away the foreign gods which are among you and incline your heart to the LORD God of Israel." They needed to now prove their sincerity by their actions. Joshua knew that many of them were practicing idolatry in secret, and he demanded that they get rid of these idols. No compromise was possible. They must either serve the Lord with all their hearts, or not at all. It was their choice. The people responded immediately "The LORD our God we will serve, and His voice we will obey" (v. 24).

Our commitment to the Lord requires us to examine our lives. The people of Israel needed to put away the idols they still cherished. We need to review our lives to identify anything that is demanding the attention and affection that belong to the Lord (Col. 3:5-6).

The People Renew the Covenant (vv. 25-28)

The people had now made a commitment to the Lord three times. So with great solemnity Joshua renewed the covenant, and wrote the agreement in the "Book of the Law of God" (v. 26). The Book in which the covenant was written may have been kept beside the ark of the covenant (cf. Deut. 31:24-27). In addition to the Book, Joshua appears to have written the words of the covenant on a large stone and set it up under the oak that was by the sanctuary in Shechem (v. 26). Archeologists have found in the Shechem area a large pillar of limestone which may possibly have been the stone that Joshua had set up.

Joshua said that the stone was to be a witness, for "it has heard all the words of the LORD which He spoke to us." He continued, "It shall therefore be a witness to you, lest you deny your God" (v. 27). This ended the covenant ceremony, and Joshua allowed the people to depart.

The Death of Joshua (vv. 29-31)

Not long after the renewal of the covenant, Joshua died. Notice he is called the son of Nun and "the servant of the LORD." He had been *Moses' servant* for forty years and the leader of the nation of Israel for about thirty years. In the conquest of Canaan he had proved that he could rightly be called the *servant of the Lord* by his dependence on Him and his obedience to Him. There is no more honored title for the child of God than to be known as a servant of God. We all should aspire to be true servants of God in all that we do, seeking to please Him, obey Him, and serve Him. Joshua was 110 years old when he died, having lived a full life. He was buried in the city that had become his inheritance, Timnath Serah (v. 30; cf. 19:50).

The people of Israel highly respected Joshua and gladly followed him as their leader as long as he lived. In following him they also served the Lord during his lifetime and the lifetimes of the elders of Israel who had been the leaders of the twelve tribes during the conquest and the settlement of the land. They were faithful because they had known the works of God, that is, they had personally witnessed the great victories that God had given them during the conquest. The book of Judges tells a different story about the next generation.

Joseph's Bones are Buried (vv. 32-33)

The second to the last verse in the book of Joshua mentions that the children of Israel buried the bones of Joseph in Shechem. Joseph had been the favored son of Jacob and the father of Ephraim and Manasseh. Joseph's dying request to his sons had been for his bones to be buried in the Promised Land. His body had been embalmed in Egypt and kept in a coffin (Gen. 50:25). In the exodus, Moses made sure that they took Joseph's bones with them (Ex. 13:19). Now, after forty years of wandering and another thirty years in Canaan, the time had come to bury them. When Jacob returned from Padan Aram to the Promised Land, he purchased a piece of land near Shechem and built an altar there (Gen. 33:18-20). It was there that they buried the bones of Joseph.

The final verse of the book reports the death of Eleazar the son of Aaron, the brother of Moses and the first high priest of Israel. Eleazar had served as the second high priest and was succeeded by his son Phinehas. Eleazar was buried on a hill that belonged to Phinehas. Commentators make the point that the priests were not supposed to own land and wonder whether the fact that Phinehas had property (even though it was gifted to him) may have been the beginning of departure from the true God.

In Conclusion

The chapter and the book conclude with three burials. First, Joshua, Israel's leader, was buried. He had finally earned the distinction of being called the "servant of the LORD." Second, the bones of Joseph, the man who prophesied (by means of visions) many different events, were finally buried. Joseph had died in Egypt at the same age Joshua was when he died. Third, Eleazar the high priest was buried (Num. 20:25-29). These three burials signified the end of an era. It was the era of Israel's national identity in which God delivered them from the bondage of Egypt, established an order for worship, and gave them a land for their possession and inheritance. These three burials foreshadow Jesus the Messiah who has risen from the dead and will one day establish Himself in all three offices held by these men Prophet (like Joseph), Priest (like Eleazer) and King (like Joshua).

A Devotional Commentary

Genesis: From
Creation to a Nation

Order Your Copy Today
Call: 1-888-338-7809
Online: www.ecsministries.org

The ECS Classic Series

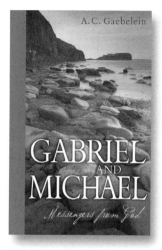

Gabriel and Michael

Kings of Israel

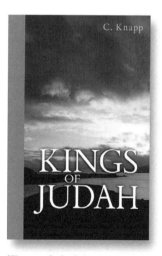

Kings of Judah

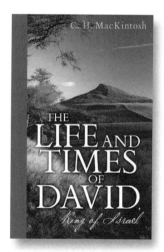

The Life and Times
of David, King of Israel

ORDER YOUR COPY TODAY
CALL: 1-888-338-7809
ONLINE: www.ecsministries.org

Faith in Action

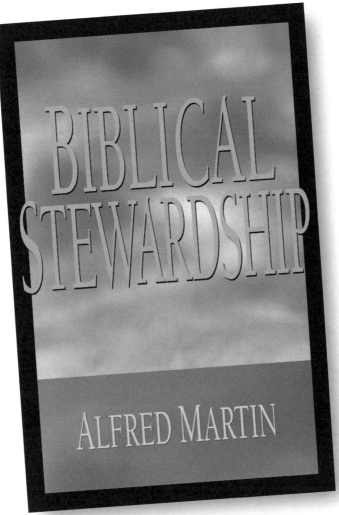

Biblical Stewardship

ORDER YOUR COPY TODAY
CALL: 1-888-338-7809
ONLINE: www.ecsministries.org

Application for Today

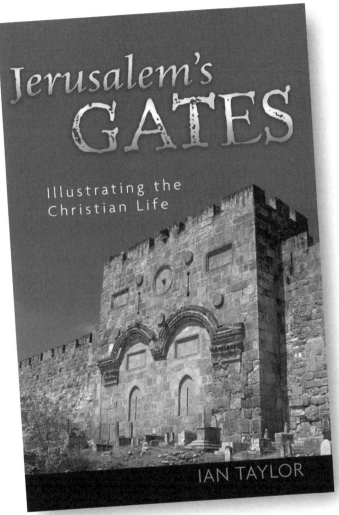

**Jerusalem's Gates:
Illustrating the Christian Life**

ORDER YOUR COPY TODAY
CALL: 1-888-338-7809
ONLINE: www.ecsministries.org

Practical Principles

Win the Battle
for Your Mind

ORDER YOUR COPY TODAY
CALL: 1-888-338-7809
ONLINE: www.ecsministries.org